Wheeling LoANeR

Also by David Shenk

Data Smog

Skeleton Key
(with Steve Silberman)

the end of patience

the end of patience

Cautionary Notes on the Information Revolution

David Shenk

This book is a publication of

Indiana University Press
601 North Morton Street
Bloomington, IN 47404-3797 USA

http://www.indiana.edu/~iupress

Telephone orders 800-842-6796
Fax orders 812-855-7931
Orders by e-mail iuporder@indiana.edu

The paper used in this publication meets the minimum requirements of American National Standard for Information Sciences–Permanence of Paper for Printed Library Materials, ANSI Z39.48-1984.

Manufactured in the United States of America

Library of Congress Cataloging-in-Publication Data

Shenk, David, date

    The end of patience : cautionary notes on the information revolution / David Shenk.
        p.   cm.
        Includes index.
        ISBN 0-253-33634-1 (cl : alk. paper)
        1. Information technology—Social aspects. 2. Telecommunication—Social aspects. 3. Information society. I. Title.
    HM851.s54 1999
    303.48'33—dc21   99-24979

1 2 3 4 5   04 03 02 01 00 99

For Alex

Contents

Prologue

The Problem with Hypertext

Someday, perhaps tens of thousands of years from now, the human form may be very different. Our eyes might point in different directions, our ears may process different channels of sound in distinct parts of the brain, and we might even talk and think in fragmented hyper-speak.

Until then, we are all stuck in a linear world. We can dabble in hyperfiction and so-called dense TV as forms of entertainment, and as thought-experiments. But let us not forget that our brains and our society are better served by *The Adventures of Huckleberry Finn* and the *New Yorker*. Our sentences work best when they have a subject, an object, and a verb. Our stories work best when they have an ending.

As we surf the Internet, we're in danger of forgetting this basic truth. With hypertext, endings are irrelevant—because no one ever gets to one. Reading gives way to surfing, a meandering, peripatetic journey through a maze of threads. The surfer creates his or her own narrative, opting for the most seductive link immediately available. As a research technique, this is superb. As a mode of thought, however, it has serious deficiencies.

Faster is not always better, and segmentation is not always smarter. If Jane Austen could see what her book *Pride and Prejudice* has become on the World Wide Web, she would faint dead away. In the first five sentences, there are four invitations to go elsewhere.

In our restless technological optimism, we tend to look down on old technologies as inferior. But we need to resist this. Some of the boring old linear technologies, including the one we're using right now, still ride on the cutting edge of human intelligence. The works of George Orwell, E. B. White, and Joan Didion read from beginning to end not just because of the primitive tools these writers used. Traditional narrative offers the reader a journey with a built-in purpose; the progression of thought is specifically designed so that the reader may learn something not just from parts of the story, but also from the story as a whole.

For all of its advantages, hypertext has no whole. As the Web becomes integrated into the fabric of our lives—mostly to our great benefit—we should employ hyperlinking as a useful tool, but be careful not to let it govern the way we think.

—Broadcast on NPR's *All Things Considered*, May 14, 1997

Introduction & Acknowledgments

There's no getting around irony sometimes. When *Data Smog* was first published, many people couldn't resist the barb: "You wrote a *book* about information overload?" Others would sarcastically apologize for "smogging" my email in-box, or beg my pardon for not promptly returning a call with the playful excuse, "Hey—I took your advice. I unplugged."

Herewith some more ammunition. This book, for which friends and critics will probably forever rib me as being "just more data smog," is a collection of essays, reportage, and dialogue from October 1996 through March 1999, the two-plus years that followed my work on *Data Smog.* As part of my continuing interest in articulating the trade-offs of technological progress, I was privileged to write columns for *Hotwired* and *MSN,* contribute commentaries to *All Things Considered, Feed, MSNBC,* the *New York Times, Salon,* and *Wired,* and publish lengthy pieces in *Harper's,* the *New Republic,* the *Nation,*

MIT's *Technology Review*, and *Atlantic Unbound*. I also gave a number of speeches throughout the United States and Japan (the latter thanks to a fellowship from the U.S.-Japan Foundation), and had the great pleasure of interacting with some of our most thoughtful and dynamic technology observers. I did all this not as a technology expert myself but as an amused, enthused, and often confused outsider, wandering among the trees while trying desperately not to lose perspective on the forest. This book captures, and in a sense concludes, that experience which *Data Smog* made possible.

Trying to discern and articulate the unwelcome consequences of information technology without losing a sense of appreciation for its many benefits has been a daily professional and personal struggle. How do we attain wisdom and meaning in a world which ceaselessly buzzes and blinks? These pieces reflect my efforts to explore this issue in some depth. Most of them, although hopefully reflective of broad social concerns, come out of very personal ones. How are my daughter and her daughter going to be affected by the flurry of images, by "smart" machines, by genetic maneuverability, by the surging free-marketization of the media and academic science? What holds these pieces together, I hope, is what might be called an "enthusiastic skepticism" for the adoption of the advanced technologies unfolding before us. While the benefits of these machines are manifest, their introduction also involves many trade-offs. To ignore them, as most marketers would apparently prefer that we do, is to invite a future of regrets.

I am grateful to my editors and producers for their intelligence and guidance: John Benditt, Brooke Shelby Biggs, Martha Brockenbrough, Jonathan Cohn, Sean Collins, Joan Connell, Eamon Dolan, Stephen Dubner, Bill Goggins, Amanda Griscom, Rob Guth, Colin Harrison, Steven Johnson, Charles Lane, Susan Lehman, Sam Lipsyte, Karen Rothmyer, Wen Stephenson, Katrina vanden Heuvel, Ellen Weiss, and zig Zeigler. I am also indebted to my superb agent/collaborator Sloan Harris, to my *technorealism* partner-in-crime Andrew Shapiro, and to the many other friends, colleagues, and strangers who have been generous with their praise, criticism, and provocative ideas. To the Apple Computer technicians in New York and Tokyo: *domo arigato gozaimasu*. To Alex and Lucy, who maintain and sometimes mend my soul, my thanks and love.

i.

the disease of images

*How the Ubiquity of Video Images
Can Subvert Culture*

[*Technology Review,* September/October 1998]

Stealing Calm

An Ode to Radio

Chances are, unless you've ever been alone in a radio booth, you have never experienced complete silence. I've had the privilege a number of times in the last few years and have come to savor it. Whenever I'm scheduled to record a commentary or defend my point of view on a talk show, I try to show up a few minutes early just to bathe in the silence of the studio. Radio booths are generally cramped and are rarely much to look at—ratty carpet, corrugated walls (designed to nullify all sound waves coming from whatever angle), soft creakless chairs. But the aural stillness lends a cathedral-like quality. There is an unnatural calm which slows down time. You can hear your own breath.

Of course, no one *listens* to radio in that kind of cocoon. We turn it on in the car, the backyard, the kitchen. But the silence of a radio booth says something important about the nature of the medium. As the delivery mechanism for a precious, fragile stream of audio, there is an uncompromising, almost militaristic component to radio's mission—that of vigilant protector. *Seal the perimeter.* Radio tightly focuses on a certain sound source to the rigid exclusion of all others. In a radio engineer's control room, there's a sanctity surrounding audio that you just don't see anywhere else in the media world. That's because with most other communications technologies, particularly anything with moving visuals, the task is not to slow down time, but to feed it as it ravenously marches forward.

I've been thinking a lot lately about the difference between radio and multimedia, wondering how it is that such a technically confined medium seems to me so intellectually superior. How does radio, with its limited bandwidth and narrow one-lane avenue of sensory impact, triumph over the audiovisual feast of television and even the World Wide Web when it comes to conveying memorable information, provocative ideas, and deeply human feeling? Marshall McLuhan wrote that radio "is really a subliminal echo chamber of magical power to touch remote and forgotten chords." I know I couldn't possibly count all the times, in ten years of daily listening to a variety of programming on National Public Radio, that I have wept, had deep spiritual epiphanies, come up with provocative story ideas, or heard an idea or perspective that fundamentally changed the way I thought about music or politics or language or science. But I do know that I owe a good bit of my life and career to what I've heard on shows like *All Things Considered, Fresh Air,* and *A Prairie Home Companion,* and I have spoken to many others who feel the same way. With no disrespect meant toward the many serious and talented practitioners of commercial and public television, TV is regrettably not a medium that regularly nourishes the spirit or challenges the mind.

A comparison with TV is particularly instructive in light of the impending televisionization of the Web. The other day I was asked to appear on CNN*fn* for a brief discussion about the cultural implications of the failure of Panamsat's now-infamous Galaxy4 satellite. Always happy to plug my book, I ironed my shirt and found my way to CNN's New York studios, near Penn Station in midtown. The differences between TV and radio were much on my mind as I arrived at the twentieth floor and began to notice that everything about the studio, from the makeup to the polished veneer set to the antiseptic dialogue on the TelePrompTers, said, "Skim the surface." I wasn't there to truly discuss information proliferation; I was there to look the part of having a discussion about information proliferation, to mimic the type of discussions that might occur if the TV cameras weren't on. The audio would provide an appropriate backdrop for the image of the anchor and me speaking, looking into each other's eyes, exchanging penetrating remarks.

I did my seven minutes. It was, like the rest of the spots I saw that morning while I waited, unmemorable. I shook hands with the anchor, thanked him. Then, as I was heading away, a funny thing happened. One of the production assistants caught up to me and said, "Hey, interesting stuff, can I ask you a question?" We proceeded to talk for another seven minutes or so about computers, the Internet, Bill Gates, and so on. It was about the same length as my conversation on the air, and infinitely more interesting. It was an actual conversation, with a life of its own that couldn't have been charted in advance.

I don't fault the anchor or the producer for the drabness of the

CNN*fn* conversation. I think the flaws are embedded in the video medium itself. There's an interesting paradox at work here: moving images capture attention but subvert thought, a condition that is perhaps most vividly illustrated in the 1991 Wim Wenders film *Until the End of the World.* Setting: It is 1999, and a scientist has just invented a camera that can record and replay not just images, but also the neurological recipe behind each image. It can enable the blind to see what sighted people see, or for anyone to replay their own dreams. Several characters in the film become hopelessly addicted to, and strung out on, an endlessly intoxicating video montage. The story is an elegy for our post-industrial society: a collection of fragmented, alienated individuals who seem to continually shift their attention between flickering images—GameBoy, flashing billboards, news and stock tickers, and so on.

Wenders calls this "the disease of images," the problem where "you have too many images around so that finally you don't see anything anymore." This in-your-face property of television becomes its defining characteristic for both producers and consumers. The inherently captivating and distracting properties of moving images allow force —TV and its practitioners to constantly acknowledge and flaunt the primacy of images over ideas. It would seem as fundamental a natural law as paper-covers-rock or scissors-cuts-paper: video trumps thought— complex thought anyway. Narratives work brilliantly on TV, of course, and the medium thrives on conveying primal feelings like lust, betrayal, and triumph. There's something about the power of the moving image, though, that not only doesn't require much intellectual effort to consume, but actually discourages such exertion. *Sit back and let me come to you.* The frozen look on any TV viewer's eyes confirms this. So does the feeling we all have when we're a bit under the weather and just want to escape; we don't turn on the radio in those instances, or pick up a book. We watch TV. It's the great escape because it does all the work for us.

This observation is reinforced by the most ambitious TV programming. In an interview not long ago, Neil Postman was asked his opinion of the *Ascent of Man* TV series, which was built around the ideas of philosopher Jacob Bronowski. As usual, Postman honed in on the essential point to be made. "Here's an interesting point about the series," he said. "If you read the book, which actually was the television script printed, you realized that Bronowski actually has a theory of social change. And almost anyone who read the book could be asked a question about whether or not they think they agree with Bronowski's theory of social change. If you would ask this question of people who only saw *Ascent of Man* on television, they would say, 'What theory?' The theory disappeared on television even though Bronowski actually uses the words that would appear in the book. Why does the theory disappear? Because the program, being good television, is filled with exotic, interesting, exciting images." Postman, of course, is author of *Amusing Ourselves to Death*, which worries that we're entertaining and distracting ourselves into cultural oblivion.

Fortunately, there is no analogous "disease of sounds." Radio producers face an entirely different set of problems. Television need only be seen to be watched. For radio, though, to be *heard* is not necessarily to be *listened to*. Though the juxtaposition of certain sounds can be comforting, inspiring, saddening, maddening, and powerful in a hundred other ways, those are all emotions of consideration. Sound moving forward in time is not inherently mesmerizing or captivating. It doesn't grab. On the contrary: the listener has to reach out with his or her attention and grab *it*, pull it in, and keep pulling with a considerable amount of focus. Television producers and webmasters have learned to speed up images as a way of seducing people to refrain from changing channels. That doesn't work in radio. String together ninety split-second fragments of nonlinear audio in the same way that MTV does with video, and you'd see many unhappy faces.

Images captivate us effortlessly, and are difficult to filter out. Screening out sounds, though, is something that humans are well constructed to do. Beginning with frequency-filter membranes in the inner ear (cochlea), we constantly discriminate between competing sounds so that we can make sense of our sound environment. This filtering, or "masking," enables us to perceive certain sounds as drowning out other sounds. Without it, the audio world would make very little sense to us.

Perhaps because it is so difficult to separate one sound from another and our auditory neurons are expressly designed to respond to this challenge, or perhaps because of other aspects of how sound is processed in our brain, we also *psychologically* discriminate among sounds. It is very easy, we all know from experience, to lose focus on what someone is saying to you in a room, even when there is very little audio competition. And it's downright common to have the radio on and stop noticing its contents altogether. As soon as we stop pulling audio in, it fades into the background.

Being able to so easily ignore radio turns out to be the luckiest thing of all for the medium, because it also means that in order to really listen to it, we must become truly engaged. Radio won't "work" in the neural background. It won't settle for an intellectual glazing over. It requires more of a commitment, a certain level of consideration, concentration, rumination. And there's a direct payoff, for the cerebral effort: studies by UCLA's Patricia Greenfield and colleagues show that radio inspires more imagination than television.

A healthy imagination and other aspects of creative thinking are the surest signs that we're pulling the information into our minds and interacting with it, that we're converting the information into knowledge. Kurt Vonnegut expressed this point marvelously in a recent magazine interview: "I can remember when TV was going to teach my children Korean and trigonometry," he said. "Rural areas wouldn't even have to have very well educated teachers; all they'd have to do is turn on the box. Well, we can see what TV really did. . . . We are not born with imagination. It has to be developed by teachers, by parents. . . . A book is an arrangement of 26 phonetic symbols, 10 numbers, and about 8 punctuation marks, and people can cast their eyes over these and envision the eruption of Mount Vesuvius or the Battle of Waterloo. But it's no longer necessary for teachers and parents to build these circuits. Now, there are professionally produced shows with great actors, very convincing sets, sound, music. And now there's the information superhighway."

Vonnegut's sarcastic rant suggests that electronic visual technologies have changed the rules somewhat. Historically, we have associated *sight* with *understanding*. "Of all the senses, trust only the sense of sight," Aristotle wrote in his *Metaphysics*. Our present language is loaded with words and phrases which make analogies between the two—"insight," "illuminate," "enlighten," "clarity," "observation," "brilliant," and so on. In an age where more and more images are in motion, though, sight can neither be trusted nor counted on to propel us into thought and action. We're going to have to recalibrate our language and our thinking for a digitized age.

Fortunately, we have abundant text and audio resources at our disposal. We have the freedom to retreat to serious radio programming, to pull into the interior of our mind, to *engage*. The sanctity of audio allows for an intellectual intimacy that can be as nourishing as we allow it to be. None of these technological parameters ensure that a great percentage of radio programming will live up to the medium's potential—there's as much titillating mindlessness available on the radio dial as there is via the television remote or the web browser. But it does set the bar high enough that an ambitious few will inevitably (and consistently) scale to great heights. I am chopping vegetables in my kitchen and listening to the first explanation of schizophrenia that has ever really made sense to me; now I am driving in my car listening to a very interesting conversation about beach erosion; now I am in the shower, really learning something about myths in Ireland. It's not just the quality of the information that's resonating with me; it's also the conduit. At its best, radio is at once formal and intimate, thoughtful and spiritual, visually confining and cerebrally expansive.

At CNN*fn*, I noticed that as I spoke informally with the production assistant, we mostly did not look at each other. We'd glance over frequently to make eye contact, to reinforce some point or some tonal cue. But most of the conversation itself was happening irrespective of the visuals—in spite of the visuals. We were intentionally avoiding a situation where our eyes would constantly be fed. On TV a moment before, it had been just the opposite. All conversation was made with lasting eye contact, perhaps the best clue of all that it wasn't a conversation but a visual simulacrum—a video painting—of a conversation.

About an hour after I left the CNN building, I was in a radio studio on 56th Street near Sixth Avenue, participating in a wonderful public radio show called *The Connection*, hosted by Christopher Lydon. For about an hour, a handful of people shared observations and ideas, spoke with their eyes metaphorically closed, making a psychic connection. Real thoughts were formed, articulated, considered. As I listened to thoughtful guests and callers, I wondered: is any technology more "interactive"? It wasn't a perfect hour. I stumbled a bit, said some things I'd wished I'd said better. But it was still a terrific conversation. Callers thanked the host for another marvelous program, and you could hear that they meant it. People weren't just listening because they had time to kill. They were engaged. This wasn't entertainment; it was nourishment.

After the show, I stuck around the studio for a few precious minutes to let the ideas settle a bit, and to steal just one more moment of calm.

[*MSN*, October 1996]

Just Sit Still

The Problem with the Java-Infused Web

Watch it wiggle, see it jiggle. After lying motionless for years and years, an interactive but nevertheless static medium, the Web is coming alive. Here I see text dancing across the screen; there I am startled by a harmless-seeming icon actively running away from my mouse arrow as the arrow approaches it; now I am being entertained by a zippy light show and a head that pops in and out of view. It's like there's a party on my screen and I'm invited. What fun.

The bells and whistles have arrived. "Applets," they're called, as in baby applications, tiny bits of software that quietly download onto your computer and proceed to transform a stone cold web page into a digital fiesta. If the Web is eye candy, these new applets are sizzling pop rocks.

Ready to walk through the looking glass? Once you've entered this world of ActiveX and Java, the Web will never be the same and neither will you. That's because these blinking, burbling, ecstatic web pages of new make the old, stiff-as-a-board web pages seem very '80s. The inactive virtual landscape is a barren, desolate prairie, with not so much as a tumbleweed rolling across the land. It's as if you finally found the hoppin' bar and everyone disappeared out the back way.

One of the new active-site software companies, Shockwave, has a slogan: "Friends don't let friends build static web pages." So begins the two-tiered Web world:—the silent and the stereo, the muted and the vibrant, the "interesting" and the *wow*.

Why am I upset about this new wonder-Web? Because once upon a time, the Web seemed like a place of great intellectual promise, where minds all over the world could come together and share old ideas, spark new ideas, rev up the other 94 percent of their brain cells and take us all somewhere new. The hyperlinks, photos, icons, and formatted text were not gratuitous graphics. They were visual aids, there to assist our neural adventures.

Now we know better than to hope for such an intellectual awakening. Now we know that this is TV: The Next Generation. Kids will log on and go straight to the razzmatazz. How long will anyone sit still for the pages that don't do a song and dance? In six months how many bookmarks will mark the web pages with the real ideas, the personal expressions, the jam-packed reference pages, the home pages where people bare their souls? Few, I predict.

Now we see that the simple iconic graphics and formatting that made the Web "user-friendly" à la Macintosh and Windows were just a prelude to graphics that have an entirely different agenda. Like TV, our eyes will try to follow all the dancing lights and will fall into the pulsing rhythms and will quickly become transfixed; at this point, our mouths will open just a little, signifying that all thought has ceased and we have entered the infotainment zone.

ii.

when more is less

New Levels of Confusion and Incivility

[*Salon*, June 23, 1997]

The Devolution Has Been Televised

Crossfire *Turns 15: An Appreciation*

It would be difficult to say whether or not *Crossfire* is the *perfect* showcase for all that is wrong with Washington politics. It does have such an impressive blend of needless posturing, gratuitous bluster, and endless statistical slingshots. Most importantly, the show thrives on the conceit that intricate policy debates and profound social issues are best explored in short, sharp, shocking sound barks.

After fifteen years, the show may no longer be the headquarters for inflammatory polemic, but without a doubt *Crossfire* was, along with *The McLaughlin Group*, an important pioneer of the bark genre. The show bills itself as "the classic Washington political debate program," and it is hard to imagine that something as incendiary as *Rush Limbaugh*, for instance, could have existed without these trailblazers of televised unpleasantness.

That we've gotten used to the acid splashing is probably the worst news of all. Sadly, *Crossfire* no longer irks or offends. We've become inured to the rhetorical and statistical free-for-alls cascading over the radio, television, and even the Internet. *Crossfire* is no longer simply the enemy; *Crossfire* is now us.

Crossfire ushered in a new era of what former *From the Left* anchor Michael Kinsley once aptly called "Stat Wars." We could pin blame on founding producer Randy Douthit, or founding hosts Tom Braden and Pat Buchanan, or even Ted Turner. But the truth is that such a staging was probably inevitable. Since the early '70s, the statistical and rhetorical ammunition that fuels *Crossfire* and the rest of on-air Washington had been piling up, manufactured by hundreds of so-called "think tanks," institutions with purposefully vague and formidable names like Institute for Responsive Government and National Center for Policy Analysis. Staffed with some of the most skilled polemicists and statisticians in the land and generously supported by corporations with specific political agendas, their task is to produce mountains of data to support partisan policy objectives.

These institutions are masters of contention. A good many of them are expressly uninterested in an earnest pursuit of the truth. "We're not here to be some kind of Ph.D. committee giving equal time," Burton Pines, then a vice president of the right-wing Heritage Foundation, said years ago. "Our role is to provide conservative public-policy makers with arguments to bolster our side. We're not troubled over this. There are plenty of think tanks on the other side."

In fact, the think tank field is dominated by corporate money and conservative political philosophy. But it is true that, whatever position you might like to argue, there is an impressive mound of data in support of your position only a fax machine away. The top-caliber *Crossfire* participants know how to access this data and turn it into a verbal machine-gun nest. Observe the masters at work:

PAT BUCHANAN, *Co-host:* Arkansas was fourth highest in teen pregnancy when [Dr. Joycelyn Elders] took over. Now, it's second or first. Under her program of condom distribution and the rest, STDs, sexually transmitted diseases, the incidence of them have soared . . .

DR. WALTER FAGGETT, *National Medical Association:* You take it out of context, Pat. That's the problem. Again, the teenage pregnancy rate in Arkansas—the rate of increase has decreased.

MICHAEL KINSLEY, *Co-host:* And the rate of increase in Arkansas is lower than the rate of increase in the rest of the country.

RALPH REED, *The Christian Coalition:* No, it isn't. Between 1987 and 1992, teen pregnancy increased in Arkansas by fifteen percent, at the time that it was increasing at five percent at the national average. It's gotten a lot worse.

MICHAEL KINSLEY: The statistic I saw was seventeen percent in Arkansas, but it was eighteen percent in the country.

—from 7/16/93

We the audience are, of course, entertained by the barrage. And also stunned: the statistical anarchy freezes us in our cerebral tracks. The psychological reaction to such an overabundance of information and competing expert opinions is to simply avoid coming to conclusions. "You can't choose any one study, any one voice, any one spokesperson for a point of view," explains psychologist Robert Cialdini. "So what do you do? It turns out that the answer is: you don't do anything. *You reserve judgment.* You wait and see what the predominance of opinion evolves to be."

"But," Cialdini continues, confronting the paradox, "I don't know that we have the luxury to wait that long, in modern life."

We may not, but that's not executive producer Rick Davis's problem. All he has to do is carry us for thirty minutes. "From the Right, I'm Cold-Hearted Conservative." "From the Left, I'm Knee-Jerk Liberal." As American politics has struggled to break out of these strictures, particularly since the end of the Cold War, *Crossfire* and its cousins have, for the sake of clarity, for the sake of character-driven entertainment, sharply reinforced the notion of us vs. them. Their message is: Despite what you might read in the *Washington Monthly* or *The New Republic*, or from what you may hear from Bill Clinton or Bill Bradley, there is no interesting new middle ground, no important "conversation." You're either fer us or agin us. The *Crossfire* bluster is designed expressly to exploit and even to widen the divide — great for producers, terrible for democracy.

And the acrimony is, of course, purely synthetic. "The viewer might think you're ready to strangle each other," Robert Novak, who works for CNN's *Capitol Gang*, told Tad Friend for a recent *New York Times Magazine* piece on punditry. "But the heat is done for television. It's a little like professional wrestling."

A little like professional wrestling. *(I'm coming after YOU, Sununu!)* Need anything more be said? For the enrichment of Time Warner Turner stockholders, *Crossfire* gleefully passes over the Agora in favor of the Coliseum. Not only does it consistently reduce issues of great importance to well-lighted mudslinging. It also provides an ideal off-season campaign platform for America's great contemporary Holocaust-revisionist, Pat Buchanan.

Happy anniversary, *Crossfire.* I don't suppose you could just go away now?

[*Wired*, February 1997]

More Is Less

How Faster News Can Hurt Journalism

With the introduction of Pointcast, MSNBC, and myriad other instant electronic news services, 1996 turned out to be the best year yet for news junkies. And this is just the beginning. The Internet and telcom deregulation have spawned a news revolution that will make today's flurry of instantaneous news look like a scene from *The Flintstones*.

What's good for Ted Turner and Bill Gates isn't all that great for the rest of us, however. In a world glutted with information, constant updates are not only a diminishing asset; they are becoming a dangerous distraction. Watching could be hazardous to the health of human civilization. Since the dawn of time, humans have been constructing a quilt of community understanding out of *new* information, gathered and passed around. In a world of information scarcity, messenger/ journalists performed the vital community service of acquiring and transmitting fresh data. Newspapers, wrote Arthur Young in 1793, are "that universal circulation of intelligence which in England transmits the last vibration of feeling or alarm, with electric sensibility, from one end of the Kingdom to another." This sentiment was echoed by Adolph Ochs when he bought *The New York Times* in 1896. Its mission, he declared, was to "give the news, all the news . . . and give it as early, if not earlier, than can be learned through any other reliable medium."

But something funny happened on the way to journalistic excellence: information came into abundance. First, cameras put us on the scene, and now email has allowed ordinary citizens to scoop reporters. Data is so plentiful, in fact, that consumers face the curious hazard of information glut. We cannot keep up with the information we produce.

In this context, new information becomes more of a diversion than a contribution to society. Today's informational challenge is to manage and share the vast quantities of information we already have stored up. News is not, of course, completely irrelevant; we will always need to stay abreast of local, national, and world affairs. But the value of daily updates will pale in comparison to information we already have on hand—how to feed and clothe ourselves, fight pestilence, and govern ourselves using a balance of strict laws and broad liberties. The new challenge is to share this information with one another, to manage it thoughtfully, and transform it into knowledge inside millions of individual brains. This is not so much fact hunting as it is data gardening.

The traditional news media haven't come to terms with this fundamental shift, which is why Yahoo, AltaVista, and the other web libraries are fast becoming our primary information sources. Yet old-school reporters and editors maintain a fierce bias against what they call old news. "We've *covered* that," they snarl. "It's been done." They opt instead *for anything that smells new or dramatic:* opinion polls, trial testimony, celebrity marriages, divorces, disgraces, deaths. "My job is not to educate the public," insists television producer Steve Friedman in a typically myopic declaration of journalistic principle. "My job is to tell the public what's going on."

His distinction is critical. Mere telling focuses on the mechanics of transmitting information of the moment, while education assumes a responsibility for making sure that knowledge sticks. Journalists who limit their role to news flashes are absolving themselves of any overarching obligation to the audience. In our new world, reporters must become more like teachers, and we all must learn the skills of the librarian. Information management is the fuel for our thriving civilization. But in just the last fifty years, the integrity of our data management has been threatened by a historical first: production of information is now dramatically outpacing consumption. This leaves us with what Finnish sociologist Jaako Lehtonen calls an "information discrepancy," a permanent processing deficit. "The real issue for future technology," says Columbia University's Eli Noam, "does not appear to be production of information, and certainly not transmission. Almost anybody can add information. The difficult question is how to reduce it."

If we can't find a way, Noam warns, we may be setting ourselves on a road toward a chaos that not even scientists will enjoy observing. The second law of thermodynamics dictates that eventually the world will lose its energy potential and peter out. The organization of information, says Noam, is the one major counterforce to entropy. Not being able to effectively manage our information—lagging badly behind in the processing/sharing—means that we may be beginning to lose control of information and finally succumbing to entropy. In this light, an increasingly news-manic culture is not only less and less attuned to its own needs, but may also be on a track to oblivion. Now *that's* devolution.

[*MSN*, October 1996]

A Wrinkle in Cyberspace

The Unreliability of Information on the Web

> She looked over at Mrs. Which.
> Mrs. Which was there and then she wasn't.
> —*A Wrinkle in Time*, Madeline L'Engle

Imagine a map of the planet Earth converted into a land-map of web sites; instead of small red dots for each city, there are millions of tiny red lights representing the physical locality of each web site—a few thousand lights scattered over Australia, several million concentrated around San Francisco Bay, and so on. Of course, in cyberspace, it doesn't matter where these web servers are, because your computer retrieves their images and brings them right to your desktop. Remember the "location, location, location" mantra of real estate professionals? The most wonderful thing about the communications revolution is that it renders location obsolete.

Indulge me for a moment, though. Stay with this mental image of our cyberspace land map. Just a few seconds go by, and as they do the map changes radically. Thousands of new lights (web sites) come online from all over the world, while thousands of other lights go dead. On and off they go, like fireflies.

> Cannot retrieve http://fur.rscc.cc.tn.us/OWL/Clarity.html.
>
> Netscape's network connection was refused by the server www.mojuan.com
>
> 404 Not Found The requested URL/19960418/ RTRInternational-Korea.html was not found on this server

Without warning, some of your favorite web pages become invisible. Will these sites be accessible in an hour? Tomorrow? It's anybody's guess. From the perspective of the web surfer, the suddenly offline sites have entered what writer Madeleine L'Engle calls "a wrinkle in time." "There was a gust of wind and a great thrust and a sharp shattering as

she was shoved through—what? Then darkness; silence; nothing-
ness."

If the sites do return, they may not look the same. They might not
even contain the same information. In cyberspace, everything is
subject to change without warning. If you're hoping to refer back to
something you've seen before, or pass on a tip to a colleague, cross your
fingers. Web pages come and go as sponsors please, proving that the
Web is not yet the electronic library that many have declared it to be.
Instead, the Web right now is nothing more than a repository of
convenience.

Here's where location begins to matter. Take a look over your
shoulder at your office bookshelf. Have any books flown away in the
last few hours? Has any document in your filing cabinet suddenly
altered its contents? What about your local library? Has it suddenly
grown wings and hopped across town, or disappeared from view for a
few days? It's easy to take information for granted until it vanishes.

A moment of truth is coming soon for denizens of cyberspace. At
some point in the not too distant future, we're going to have to decide
if we want the Web to be a reliable conduit for the advancement of
human civilization, or whether we're content to see it become merely
the apogee of infotainment. Will the Net become the fulfillment of
H. G. Wells's "World Brain" prophecy (a "standing editorial organization . . . the mental background of every intelligent man in the
world"), or will it emerge as cable TV's wildly erratic (albeit much
more interesting) younger brother?

The matter may not be entirely up to us, I admit, but that doesn't
mean we shouldn't address it with some diligence. We might begin
with the problem of disappearing information. The firefly effect is part
of what dooms the Web to forever be a second-class institution.

What we desperately need now is organization and, yes, centraliza-
tion. Some sort of uniform card-catalog-type system is in order, to
document what comes on the web, when it leaves, when pages are
altered, and so on.

The digerati will despise this suggestion. *Impose order on the web?
Never! Information wants to be free* . . . etc., etc. But what humankind
wants is some order of reliability—information that can be shared and
ordered and put into context and found whenever it is searched for. If

information is to become our new currency, our information society must include some of the stability and reliability that we expect of all infrastructure. We must be secure that whole bodies of information won't blip on and off like fireflies. "Look Dad, I caught a web site — hey, where'd it go?"

[*All Things Considered* and *Hotwired,* September 1997]

The World Wide Library
An Immodest Proposal

There is much ado these days concerning the preservation of the Web for future historians. Microsoft's Nathan Myhrvold, WAIS's Brewster Kahle, and others are making the case that since most of the information on the Web is fleeting (the average document lasts seventy-five days, according to Kahle), it is vital that we take frequent archival snapshots.

They are right, of course. It will be invaluable for historians fifty and five hundred years from now to surf the Web as it existed in 1997. We have at least that much of an obligation to future generations.

But we also have an obligation to scholars of today. There's something missing, I believe, from the Myhrvold-Kahle exhortation to treat the Web as a conspicuous intellectual resource. What's missing is the World Wide Library.

The World Wide Library is (will be) a regimented, filtered, ultra-reliable segment of the World Wide Web. What the WWW is to society—a cheap, frictionless, ageographical counterpart—the WWL will be to libraries. All of the great (and not so great) physical libraries of the world will come together to share the holdings (as well as the costs) of one enormous virtual library. Eventually, the WWL will comprise digitized versions of the voluminous paper holdings (http://wwl.shakespeare.twelfth_night.lib). But for now, it will simply contain all *worthwhile* electronic documents.

Emphasis on *worthwhile.* Some Web purists will perhaps become inflamed by my proposition that, for purposes of research and scholarship, some sites have more credibility and value than others. I'm not just talking about the ones that can be screened out with the key phrase "pet me." In our culture, there is a critical difference between entertainment and education, and though many information providers today profit handsomely by blurring that distinction (with "infotainment" and "edutainment"—a subject for a future column), the distinction is still an important one to make.

There's a good reason, in other words, why we don't allow fifty-seven channels of cable television or billboard advertisements into conventional libraries and schools. It's the same reason why even well-endowed libraries are choosy about which books and periodicals are allowed into the system. The reason is, we construct our intellectual infrastructure on a foundation of critical thinking and discrimination. We better ourselves by learning how to say "no."

So: Online dissertations on Faulkner are allowed into the WWL; online video arcades are not; Human Genome Project reports are allowed in; sidewalk.com is not. The *New York Times* review of my book *Data Smog* is allowed in; the online HarperCollins advertisement for my book is not. The WWL will also screen for redundancy. There won't be twelve sites offering local weather updates when just one will do.

Order is another essential component in the serious exchange of ideas. Yahoo may work well as a casual guide to the online smorgasbord; it does not suffice as an online card catalog for people who would use the web as a library. The WWL will ruthlessly organize the documents it admits. When a researcher types "weather" into the WWL search engine, she won't get sixteen thousand hits. She will get one hit: the "Weather" file, which will contain the subfiles "history of," "science of," "literature on," and "current weather reports."

If she types in "rain" or "precipitation" or "tornado," she will not get a listing of every document that mentions these words. Instead, she will get the "Weather" file, followed by any relevant subfiles and sub-subfiles. The point is that structure matters. Libraries not only help us find things; they also benevolently force upon us common principles of organization.

The WWL, in other words, is the methodical, disciplined yang to the WWW's psychedelically chaotic yin. Not only will all WWL documents be organized; they will also be dated and sourced in a unified manner. On the upper left corner of every document admitted to the WWL will be the original date of publication, all dates of modification, the designer's name, the document's source of funding, and the name of the actual person taking responsibility for the information contained therein.

Also, all WWL documents will be permanent so that researchers can revisit the document as many times and for as many years as they wish, and so that—this is absolutely crucial—writers can use WWL citations in their work with the assurance that the electronic cites will stand the test of time. For example, if I wanted to write a book about Bill Gates's buying spree of the digital rights to many important historical works of art, I would need to cite Steve Silberman's terrific "Packet" column, which details how Gates bought Allen Ginsberg's "Howl."

I would propose Silberman's article for inclusion in the WWL (if it weren't already included), and, rather than cite the probably-impermanent *Hotwired* URL, cite the permanent WWL URL. Fifty years from now, my great-grandchild the technology historian could read my book and follow my cite to Steve's original article online.

My WWL proposal is not meant to be an argument for keeping full-scale Web access out of public libraries. In addition to being founts of scholarship, public libraries serve a crucial civic function: they allow people without many resources to take advantage of the plethora of news, art, entertainment, and commerce. Let the separate discussion continue about how best to provide Web access to the needy.

But let us not become distracted from this other important matter of how to finally achieve what H. G. Wells envisioned a half century ago as the "World Brain." It would be, wrote Wells, "a standing editorial organization . . . [that] would be the mental background of every intelligent man in the world. It would be alive and growing and changing continually under revision, extension and replacement from the original thinkers in the world everywhere."

For all of its virtues, the Web is not the World Brain that Wells imagined. Nor is it likely to become so in the future. But the World Brain is within our grasp. A well-trained staff of cyber-librarians will sift through the Web and produce it for us. This won't come for free, of course. But whatever the annual cost—$10 million?—the global sharing of the costs and global reaping of its rewards will make the WWL an astonishing bang for the buck. The time is now. A grand opportunity stands before us. Let us seize it.

The Mother of All Howard Sterns

Where Shock-Jock Culture Comes From

I was riding in a taxi the other day, listening to Howard Stern boast about his bulging box office receipts for the movie *Private Parts*. He is, indeed, for the time being, "King of All Media," and if you listen to him for ten minutes, you'll also hear him boast about how he has blazed the trail for rude big-mouths everywhere. Now, he's right that sleaze media is ubiquitous these days. People like Dennis Rodman and Rush Limbaugh have made wildly successful careers out of being abusive and crude. And if you go behind the scenes, the list of TV and movie producers resorting to lewd and violent content for big profit is very long indeed.

But Stern is not the real father of shock-media. Strange as it may seem, it is information technology that lies at the heart of what moralist William Bennett calls the "coarsening of our culture."

What Bennett attributes to a crisis in family values is actually a nasty side effect of the information revolution. We're bombarded today with information and stimulus like never before in history. Images are faster, sounds are louder, and data are endless and constant. A type of data smog has enveloped us, creating a new ethos within which we live and work.

In 1970, psychologist Stanley Milgram demonstrated that increases in stimulus cause people to rigorously block out all sorts of information in order to maintain their peace of mind. Milgram's laboratory at the time was the city, but thanks to information technology, the high-stim conditions he observed then are now everywhere — communication devices and advertisements now follow us wherever we go, and consequently, we have learned to zealously narrow our focus and ignore much of the stimulus barrage.

But that's only half the story. In response to our blocking techniques, marketers instinctively crank up the volume, brighten the neon, and shock people into paying attention. As the competition heats up, people do what they have to do to make their voices heard.

They TALK LOUDER. They wear more vibrant color. They show more cleavage—if they can. They say shocking things.

In the immediate sense, pumping up the volume is an effective solution. More broadly, though, it becomes part of the problem, feeding a vicious spiral in which the data smog gets thicker and thicker and the efforts to cut through the smog get ever more desperate. As the people of Earth collectively try to rise above the noise, they unwittingly create more of it. The volume and vulgarity increase notch by notch, alongside the glut.

In a more serene environment, Howard Stern, Rush Limbaugh, and all the other shock-celebrities would likely be brushed off as social misfits. In our information-glutted society, they are heroes simply for their ability to command attention. It's a terribly disturbing trend, and one that won't be stopped by books on virtues or program ratings. If we want to get rid of the purveyors of sleaze, we'll first have to reduce the data smog that fuels their livelihood.

[*The Filter,* journal of the Berkman Center for Internet and Society at Harvard Law School, October 15, 1998]

Disclose Disclose Disclose

What Newt Gingrich Doesn't Get
About the Information Revolution

This week the public is 60,000 pages and 240 video-minutes richer with information about President Clinton's relationship with Monica Lewinsky, and Newt Gingrich can proudly declare that he has fulfilled his self-willed Congressional mandate of maximum public disclosure. It would seem that Gingrich fancies himself the anti-Clinton. Whereas Clinton's cowardly credo was (allegedly) "deny, deny, deny," Gingrich's is "disclose, disclose, disclose."

But a recent *New York Times* poll shows that a majority of Americans disapprove of the release of the full Starr Report—revealing that ordinary citizens understand something about information proliferation that Congressional Republicans apparently do not. An unrestricted flood of information can sometimes be more onerous than beneficial. One of the dangers is that we will be exposed to so much data so quickly that we'll lose perspective on what it means. We'll see many trees in great detail, but have no idea what the forest looks like.

In the case of the Starr Report, it's of course titillating to hear all the details about Clinton's tryst. But we would probably all have been better served by a credible, authenticated summary. In fact, if Clinton survives, it may turn out to be *because* of the full-release; I believe a summary would have been more politically damaging by keeping a tight focus on his abuse of office. No country, not even the United States, is going to demand the resignation of a president for pleasuring a woman with a cigar.

In truth, the issue of release is a delicate question of competing virtues—the obvious virtue of public disclosure versus the equally compelling virtues of privacy, propriety, and *editing.* Responsibly editing enormous volumes of data down to digestible, contextual chunks is one of the most valuable services that human beings perform for other human beings. Gingrich, who likes to think of himself as someone who contemplates deep truths about how information works in a free society, has somehow missed this one.

Unfortunately, disclosure mania isn't limited to this one scandal. There is a disturbing presumption right now in national political circles, spirited by Gingrich, Kentucky Republican Mitch McConnell, and others, that ensuring full disclosure—"sunlight"—is the most important (and often the only) way to serve the polity. McConnell has been trumpeting a version of campaign finance legislation that mandates full disclosure of political contributions, and does nothing else.

This is not the stuff of real leadership or governance, but the abdication of it. Which means that our dazzling communications infrastructure is not being employed here as a tool to revive democracy, but as a weapon to subvert the public interest.

Ad Creep

Excerpts from an E-dialogue with Steven Johnson

This was prompted by Johnson's essay "All Kinds of Places Are Good for Ads," published in Feed *in December 1998. Steven is co-founder and editor-in-chief of* Feed *and author of* Interface Culture: How New Technology Transforms the Way We Create and Communicate. *He is also a friend, and one of my very favorite writers and thinkers. But he has stubbornly refused to be won over by my arguments about the dangers of information proliferation. We frequently joust on the subject, and he graciously allowed me to reprint one of our email debates here.*

From Johnson's essay:
   . . . Because the web is a new medium, and because many of us can still remember what it was like in the days before banners started appearing everywhere, the advertising still seems like an intrusion. Perhaps we will go through a comparable process of acclimation to the idea of advertising-supported productivity applications: at first we'll be appalled, but slowly we'll grow accustomed to those flickering images in the corner of the screen—particularly if they make the software cheaper to buy.

Thu, 17 Dec 1998 09:51:35
To: Steven Johnson <stevenj@feedmag.com>
From: David Shenk <dshenk@bigfoot.com>

Steven—I enjoyed your essay on banner-ad acclimation. . . . Isn't the real issue, though, not *whether* we will become socially acclimated to the new flicker—but what happens to us as we do become acclimated? . . . The real damage is done not when we resist the onslaught, but as we adapt to it.

Thu, 17 Dec 1998 11:10:53
To: David Shenk <dshenk@bigfoot.com>
From: Steven Johnson <stevenj@feedmag.com>

Thanks for the kind words. . . . What about this damage? If it's just a matter of acclimation to excess stimuli, then I think at a certain point you have to say—either we've acclimated or we haven't . . . If we haven't really acclimated, and something in us is still rebelling against the onslaught, then that's something to be concerned about. But what is that something?

Sat, 19 Dec 1998 23:17:23
To: Steven Johnson <stevenj@feedmag.com>
From: David Shenk <dshenk@bigfoot.com>

The way you describe it, it's as though acclimating/not acclimating is a simple binary matter. That flies in the face of what acclimation/adaptation is—substantive change. If all you want to do is scratch the surface, it's perfectly apt to ask whether an organism has or has not adapted to a new environment. Did your goldfish adjust to the backyard pond? Did your dad get used to the altitude in the Rocky Mountains? If both the fish and the father live on, we can report, as a synopsis, that they have acclimated.

But the whole story is a lot more interesting and complex: the fish that moves from the 72-degree fishbowl to the 35-degree pond goes through some pretty dramatic circulatory changes, and so does the old man on the mountain. To compensate for the lower barometric pressure at 9,000 feet, he must breathe more and deeper. His heart and lungs work much harder, his blood pressure increases . . .

So it is with increased ad-flicker and ad-clutter. We *can* adapt, no question. But that adaptation is going to set in motion a rather complex set of changes, not just—flip a switch—an advanced new ability to take in more information faster. As we go to higher info altitudes, where the information moves faster and the content/ad ratio is lower, our eyes, ears, and cerebral cortexes have more to keep up with. We do keep up, but in order to do so we habituate ourselves to shorter moments of concentration; to more concise content that "cuts to the quick"; and to a manic routine of "multitasking" which so often leads to half-baked ideas and performance.

And yes, we lose quiet moments, moments of reflection. We have fewer opportunities—and less patience—to lose ourselves in an essay or a conversation or a complex thought.

What is the price we pay for watching ads? Take the mundane example of movies shown on network TV. To see a movie for free is nice, but I think by now we all recognize that there is something qualitatively different in a movie that is shown with commercial interruptions from one with no interruptions. First, the commercial interrupts the flow. Second, it diverts our attention to a message artfully designed to trigger a distinct emotional response. Whether it "ruins" a movie or not is up to each viewer to decide. But we can all agree that there is a significant trade-off involved. We allow ourselves to be subject to distraction in return for the free media. In other words, the "fee" we pay for this content is not in dollars, but in our attention.

In a less dramatic way, we pay the same sort of attention fee with all ad-supported media. Considering that our attention is the most precious resource we have, I would argue that the fee is substantial. We're not just leasing our eyeballs to advertisers. We're leasing our consciousness.

Sun, 20 Dec 1998 23:54:27
To: David Shenk <dshenk@bigfoot.com>
From: Steven Johnson <stevenj@feedmag.com>

I actually think movies are a great illustration of what you're overlooking here—the amazing ability of the human mind to process (or at least filter out) huge quantities of information. To me, this argument always seems to get back to historical questions. Sure, it taxes us to take in the sales pitches during the commercial breaks, and it probably taxes us even more to deal with the fact that there are breaks in the narrative at all. It's a simpler world without all those advertisements, no doubt.

But to me, the relevant question is not: do the ads create more complexity for us to deal with? The question is: how do the ads compare to the movies themselves? A hundred years ago, you could have just as easily argued that the human perceptual system wasn't designed to take in the shocks and intensity and excess stimulus of high-drama cinematic entertainment, and that sitting around in the movie house watching the trains come in was bound to short out the perceptual circuits of movie freaks everywhere. I think it's reasonable to say that the sensory overload introduced by movies was far more intense than that introduced by the interruptions of ads. And yet here we are (or here *you* are) talking about the damage done by interrupting the flow of movie entertainment—as though that flow were incontestably a good thing, or at least a normal thing, measured by the standards of the human mind's basic wiring.

The world without movies was a simpler world, too, and it required an adaptive response from the movie-going audience to deal with the increased complexity of movie-going life. . . . But if movies didn't overload our perceptual systems, then I really doubt the Frito-Lay ads are going to do it.

Mon, 21 Dec 1998 12:44:58
To: Steven Johnson <stevenj@feedmag.com>
From: David Shenk <dshenk@bigfoot.com>

The historical argument is a bit of a diversion, because I'm not arguing that either new media or advertising is going to "short out" our "perceptual circuits," just as I would never argue that radio, television, and movies (or typeset or alphabet) weren't each a shocking and radical new stimulus delivery device requiring much adaptation. . . .

Again, though, I think you're portraying the issue as a stark dichotomy when I'm trying to present this as a matter of adjustments and important trade-offs. (I know I've been guilty of the same thing; there are moments in *Data Smog* where it may appear that I'm arguing that there is a certain information-overload rubicon in each brain which, once crossed, allows the mind to be inundated with stress and confusion.)

There's so much we agree on here. We agree that the mind's extraordinary wiring is such that we can adapt, and adapt beautifully, to new stimuli and complexity. We also agree that a more complex media landscape often brings marvelous benefits. I think we also agree that there are drawbacks involved.

Where I think we disagree is on the seriousness of the drawbacks.

When you invoke "the amazing ability of the human mind to process (or at least filter out) huge quantities of information," your words seem to take on somewhat of a religious quality, as though all we have to do is have faith in the extraordinary nature of the mind and all will be right. Surely, the human mind can take anything we can throw at it.

I suggest that the mind is as vulnerable as it is potent. Demagoguery and sensationalism and vulgarity and innuendo can thwart skeptical thought, can interrupt and even corrupt logical and intelligent ideas. Will a lousy potato chip ad get in the way of proper appreciation of a Steven Johnson essay? It depends on the presentation, of course. A blinking ad is going to interfere with a reader's concentration more than a static ad. An ad with a naked woman lying on a potato chip— or, to take a more realistic example (and one not dissimilar from many current banner ads on the web), an ad with the slogan "HOT SEX AND POTATO CHIPS . . . well, we'll supply the potato chips"—is going to interfere with my concentration more than a cute furry bear gnawing at a chip.

In small and large ways, letting ads creep into every corner of our lives is going to interfere with what we hold dear. I don't know anyone who thinks that Mercedes-Benz actually *ruined* championship tennis by putting their obnoxious icon on both sides of the net. But the distraction does slice away just a bit from the elegance of the game, and for the same reason I don't want to see a Nike swoosh on my pine rocking chair or on the side of the Chrysler building. Can we adjust to the Mercedes tennis net? Sure, I already have. But that doesn't mean I think it's entirely benign.

We do filter quite well—I agree with you there. But we mustn't presume that stuff we filter "out" literally stays outside of our brains without any effect on us. Filtering is not only somewhat distracting in itself; it also inevitably diverts stimuli away from our conscious and into to our unconscious minds, where most good ads are designed to work most effectively.

Why don't books have banner ads? Before we finish writing them, they probably will. Our books will sell for $4 instead of $20. I will be delighted to see that more people have my books on their shelves. But I will also feel a loss, and I suspect you will too.

Tue, 29 Dec 1998 22:35:28
To: David Shenk <dshenk@bigfoot.com>
From: Steven Johnson <stevenj@feedmag.com>

I agree much more with your thoughts here. This is the direction I was
hoping we were going, concentrating more on the semiotic coding or
the values implicit in all advertising, and less on the question of pure
stimulus and sensory overload. "Demagoguery and sensationalism
and vulgarity and innuendo" are all problems characteristic of most
modern advertising, but they are different problems from the sort
implied by your analogy to the fish and the mountaineer.

When you talk about environmental changes demanding changes
in circulatory systems or oxygen levels in the bloodstream, it really
implies that there's some kind of physiological challenge posed by
advertising, which I think is not plausible, given our skills at dealing
with much more intense stimuli. But if we're talking about the *values*
implicit in ads—and not just the smog they create—then I'm with you.
Only I think the better analogy would be to people raised in dramatically different social environments: communes, say, versus inner cit-
ies. Both environments are bound to endow the residents with distinc-
tive value systems, just as the billboarded universe of today is bound to
instill certain values in us, without our fully realizing it. (The first
value it's likely to instill is a general acceptance of the fact that ads are
everywhere.)

The next question, then, is what's wrong with the value system of
advertising? The old-school left critique used to be that it naturalized
the social construct of the market economy, but for those of us who
don't have a ready-made alternative to capitalism at hand, those values
seem hard to object to. Maybe, as you seem to imply, it's that the ads
are simply too crass and duplicitous, and thus they clog up the
infosphere with cheap messages that are a waste of our time. That's
probably true enough, though it seems clear to me that few cultural
forms in recent years have complexified with the speed and rate of
innovation of po-mo advertising. (Pop music in the sixties is the closest
analog, I think.) Most of the advertising you see on network TV these
days is at least as entertaining as the "real" content, and in the case of
the music video, it *is* the real content. And why shouldn't this be the
case? Artists have been selling their own stuff since the days of classical

patronage (and before). Is it really so offensive to have them creating interesting work that also happens to sell other people's stuff? Even if that stuff is sneakers?

I'm playing devil's advocate here, but I think it's a real question.

———

Wed, 30 Dec 1998 12:29:22
To: Steven Johnson <stevenj@feedmag.com>
From: David Shenk <dshenk@bigfoot.com>

I think we've pretty well articulated the central issues involved here. I want to be clear that while I'm very interested in your questions of ad values—and would love to kick back in front of a TV sometime and deconstruct commercials with you—I do object to the wall you're trying to put up between stimulus and values. That wall doesn't exist. The medium is the message here—the culture of ads is directly related to the environment in which they appear. Form and content are developed in context—where is this ad going? what will the consumer be doing? how much time do I have to attract the consumer's attention? how much time can I hope to hold the consumer's attention? And so on. Increased sensationalism and vulgarity in today's advertising is partly a function of our high-stim surroundings—consumers are harder to reach and marketers have to ratchet up the volume to get their attention.

We began this discussion by debating what happens when we acclimate to new forms and intensities of advertising, and to their increasing ubiquity. I do think that the acclimation will involve very real psychological challenges (most psychological changes involve physiology too, but let's leave that aside). Obviously, we have the capability in our brains to make these adjustments easily, but even those easy adjustments involve important trade-offs. When we do adjust to high-stim, as I've already argued, we make significant intellectual sacrifices. There are, no doubt, some intellectual *benefits* to the intoxicating speed of information and stimulus. And of course it's a wild fun ride. But the damage is real.

iii.

the end of patience

Problems with an Excessively Speedy Culture

[*All Things Considered*, August 16, 1997]

The End of Patience

(And the Triumph of Button Smackers)

Tell me: How slow is your computer modem? Are you still crawling around with a 2400 baud? Or are you puttering along with a 9600? Perhaps you have a 14.4, which for a while seemed fast—until you saw someone else's 28.8 shoveling data twice as quickly. Don't envy your 28.8 friend too much, though—his other pal just bought a 56K. The guy with the 56K modem logs on to the Net and starts drooling when he sees an advertisement for 128K. Does this ever end?

What if I told you that there's no such thing as a fast modem, and there never will be? That's because quickness has disappeared from our culture. We now only experience degrees of slowness. With conveniences like the fax machine, email, FedEx, beepers, and so on, we've managed to compress time to such an extent that we're now painfully aware of every second that we wait for anything. Did you ever ride in an elevator with someone so impatient, the person just kept smacking one of the floor buttons over and over? We're all becoming that person, a culture of restless button smackers. The other day I was in a McDonald's that had just introduced the guaranteed-ninety-second lunch. Now *that's* fast-food. But do you think that people won't be tapping their fingers on the counter, rolling their eyes, even looking at their watches? If you're in that button-smacking frame of mind, ninety seconds can seem like an eternity.

So it goes with technology. As we speed it up, we also speed up our expectations. As long as you are psychologically running in the technology rat race, you will never, ever be winning that race—you will always be losing it. And as long as the pace of change is as blistering as it is today, many of us are stuck with the feeling of falling behind even as we stand still.

Now, Internet experts are listening to this and thinking, "This guy doesn't know what he's talking about. The Net will be as fast as TV in a matter of a few years." And that's true—it won't be long before we can download web pages as fast as we can blink. But will we then be content with the speed of information? My guess is that we won't. We already have plenty of real-time information that we seem to be losing patience for—books, for example, or any TV show that doesn't feature quaky cameras and super-quick cuts.

No—the only way to avoid becoming a button smacker is to somehow come to terms with the waiting. You stop losing the un-winnable rat race as soon as you decide to stop running in it.

The Age of Net Scoops

The Problem with Breathless Online Journalism

One hour before the jury announced that they had found Timothy McVeigh guilty of bombing the Murrah federal building in Oklahoma City, ABCnews.com, the brand new online arm of ABCNews, delivered a phenomenal scoop: they ran a headline indicating that McVeigh had been found guilty. No other news organization in the world was able to report that same information until after the jury's verdict had been read aloud an hour later.

There was only one problem. This was no scoop at all, but a terrible error, a "technical glitch," as one ABC spokesperson called it. ABCnews.com did not have any such information—they had accidentally leaked a test-headline into the public side of their online news–server. Oops—an embarrassing slip-up for a world-class news organization.

To Internet-news buffs, the blunder felt very familiar. A year and a half ago, Pathfinder, *Time* magazine's online service, announced that O.J. Simpson had been found guilty—a few minutes after the jury announced the opposite. Oops again.

Welcome to the Age of Net Scoops, where journalists are tripping all over each other to get news out as quickly as possible. Deadlines are being moved up from the end of the week or the end of the day to *right now, get it out there right now.* Things are moving so quickly that, in practical terms, there is no more room for error. Henceforth, mistakes will be corrected after the fact. We cannot realistically expect to catch them all in time.

This uncontrollable urge to transmit information as quickly as possible is not just a media virus. It infects us all. Just look at the email you receive. Every day I get notes riddled with misspellings and other sloppiness from people who not only know better, but would be mortified to read their own carelessness. I'm not talking about informal chatty writing—the style of email should be casual. I'm talking about reckless, ugly writing—a media scholar who spelled "reeally" with two e's, and a dean at a prestigious graduate school who asked me something about the "sond barrier" It's quite common to read sentences in email with key words missing. Reading these notes can become sort of a parlor game.

Of course, these are relatively harmless mistakes. But they're symbolic, I think, of the thoughtlessness that can creep into our lives when we speed it up so. Speed is also clearly a major factor in the nastiness one can encounter online. Flame wars begin when people get caught up in the heat of the moment. How many angry letters over the years have you started to write and wisely not sent? With email, the message often gets sent before you have time to reflect.

It's a strange thing to realize, but the truth is that technology can dramatically affect the way we behave. Keeping this in mind, we can try to appreciate the many benefits of speedy communication while we work to avoid some of the surprising new pitfalls.

[*MSN*, October 1996]

This Just In

The Problem with Pointcast

Did you ever try to enjoy a serene moment with a daily news reporter? It's like trying to read a novel on horseback. Newsroom veterans can't sit still. Their eyes jump around, along with their thoughts. This is because they spend long stretches of time in front of caffeinated news terminals, watching wire stories flit across the screen at the rate of several per minute. Keeping up with the ever-changing minutiae of world events is taxing. By the end of the day, these people are badly in need of aromatherapy and a hot bath.

If this sounds like fun, I've got some wonderful news: now you and your colleagues and family can plug into the constant buzz of news-wires right in the comfort of your own office or home. Find out how the President of the United States is doing—twelve times a day. Get weather updates every eight minutes. Hear about the progress of the General Motors labor negotiations thrice before lunch, and four times more before dinner. Welcome to a world where the news is always brand new. Now "boredom" is just another one of those words they used to use in the '80s—like "kinder, gentler" and "ghostbusters."

Your avenue to news nugget nirvana is to download Pointcast, the instant news update service software which works in tandem with web browsers to update your PC with headline news as often as you like. If you have a direct Internet connection, it will update automatically. Otherwise, you simply press the "update" button whenever you fancy. Pointcast also doubles as a screensaver which flashes its latest news bulletins on your screen when you're not using it for something else, bringing a quiet-yet-hypnotic CNN Lite right to your desk.

It's a nifty service, and it comes free, but followers of this column will not be surprised to learn that I am downcast about Pointcast.

I don't want to be unfair to this particular service. For what they're aiming to do, it works well (even if it is a little dizzying with its constant-motion advertisements). My problem is with the entire news nugget industry, including prominent players MSNBC, CNN*fn*, Fox-

News, Top News, and InfoJunkie. These services, and their television counterparts, provide the illusion of informing the public when in reality they are merely entertaining us.

While most of the general subjects mentioned in news updates are of great national or international importance, the actual news nuggets being reported are of little practical or intellectual value. The Dow Jones Industrial Average is up thirteen and a half points at this hour; the space shuttle's launch was scrapped due to bad weather; the jury in the O.J. Simpson trial has been selected; President Clinton declared that the Bosnian elections should go forward.

These are not by any means trivial subjects, but they contain zero educational worth when covered in news-nugget fashion. A news consumer's fundamental understanding of Bosnia or the stock market is not going to change—no matter how many news bites he or she hears about them. To actually *learn* about the subject requires not a series of updates, but a careful and thoughtful review of the situation. One long newspaper or magazine article, which would take up no more time than twenty one-minute news flashes, would do it.

But news bites are difficult to resist. In an age of very little common information, they give us a steady stream of commonality to chew on. The price we pay for this ersatz-Agora is distraction. We become like jumpy newsroom reporters. *Our* eyes dart around the room. *Our* thoughts get a bit jumbled. Now we all need aromatherapy—and we need to think hard about whether the distractions are worth it.

A Few Moments with Steve Silberman

In 1993 and 1994, Steve and I co-authored the book Skeleton Key *over a phone line, from our offices in San Francisco and New York, respectively. Email was an essential tool in our partnership. Since that time, we have both—more or less coincidentally—drifted into writing about information technology. Steve is a senior writer for* Wired News *and a contributing editor to* Wired *magazine, out of which he has built up a large and fervent fan base. His enthusiasm for* Data Smog *meant more to me than any other opinion I have come across, because of my deep admiration for his writing and because of his intimate familiarity with the subject matter. Since my book was published, we've had many provocative conversations about the personal experience of overload.*

DAVID SHENK: You and I have been in pretty close touch over the last five years, and I have watched your transition into the realm of email overload. I remember emailing you before you started getting deluged. I would send you an idea and you would reply with gusto—"hey, what a great thought, let's take it in this direction . . . " But then your replies became shorter and shorter. Now it's often a kind of a gasped, "Great idea—no time—will call—bye."

STEVE SILBERMAN: There definitely came a point where good friends could send me long emails but no longer expect to get long emails in reply. Which is perverse, because normally one would want to hear from good friends at length in any medium, and I remember just six or seven years ago, if I would get a letter from a friend it would be a momentous occasion. But now I get something like two hundred emails a day, with about eighty of them expecting an answer from me. That's a full day's work. And I have a full day's *other* work to do. The inundation of email messes with the natural gradients of intimacy in one's life.

So now I tell a lot of my close friends to call, because then I can respond in the natural rhythms of conversation. And I'm constantly aware that if I go away for three days to look at trees and clouds and to read books, I know that I'm going to come back to a thousand emails. I've wondered about what would happen if I signed off the Net for a year? Would I come back to a *million* emails? What would I do? Is this the rest of my life? Is it going to be this way forever unless I make an announcement that I'm going to become an Amish person?

I convinced my parents to get email to keep up with my sister and me. My mom is a very articulate woman. She immediately started bombarding me with four or five emails a day, and she would get offended if I didn't answer them all. I said, "Mom, sorry, but I can't answer all of these emails." Then I had to deal with her angry flames — "You told me to get email! You're being mean to your mother!" I've discovered a new type of Jewish guilt.

DS: A big part of this is changing expectations. Your mom expects quick answers to every email partly because she knows how quickly you are getting them.

SS: And I find my own expectations of others have become completely unreasonable. When I'm working on a *Wired* news story and I send someone an email, I expect to hear back within an hour or two. If that person emails me three days later and says, "Hey Steve — what's up?" I think to myself, *Oh please. You're not wired. How can you have a web site and not read your email every day?* That's not reasonable on my part, but it has become standard.

The Net makes it very easy to get work as a freelance journalist, because it's like swimming in a sea of contacts and information. So I feel like it's part of my job to be available that way. But it also has reduced the very thing that I have to offer my work which is overview, and a considered perspective. It means that much of my work consists of knee-jerk reactions to things, hastily cooked up spin. Oftentimes I have to write before I've really decided what I think about something.

I also find myself having milestone conversations with my significant other while reading email. He'll say something and I won't react right away, and he'll be like, "What's going on?" And I'll say, "I'm sorry, I just got this email." It's horrible. That's why I don't have call waiting. With call waiting, it's as if you let people into the room and then shove them out as soon as someone who might be more interesting shows up at the door. I find call waiting to be an incredibly rude institution, and I simply refuse to get it.

DS: What's the difference between call waiting and sitting in front of a terminal and being interrupted by email?

SS: There's no difference, except that call waiting is something I can decide not to have. Whereas email I *have* to have.

Recently, I discovered a solution to a problem that I didn't realize I had. My computer was crashing a lot, and just to try something out, I turned off the auto-fetch mail function on Eudora. So instead of it fetching my mail for me every ten minutes, I have to go get it myself.

As a result, I no longer have that feeling that I'm subjected to a massive force that I have no control over. It used to be like no matter what I was doing, some email might arrive that demanded my attention. That simple change gave me a modicum of a feeling of control, to make an active decision to check my mail. The other way, it's like I have a hot water faucet that I can't turn off.

iv.
the paparazzi is us

*The Control Revolution and
the Free-Marketization of Media and Science*

[*All Things Considered* and *Hotwired*, September 1997]

The Paparazzi Is Us

*How the Democratization of Media
Leads to the Tabloidization of Media*

If there's one great lesson to be gleaned from the tragedy of Princess Diana's sudden death, it's that there's a severe disconnect between the popular conception of celebrity and the lives of the celebrities themselves. Shows like *A Current Affair* and *Entertainment Tonight* specialize in transforming the mundane into the apparently glamorous, as though these people live fairy-tale lives. And, to be sure, celebrities benefit from that hype—they sell lots of books and movie tickets. But they are also haunted by it. There's nothing sexy about people rifling through your garbage and taping your phone conversations, about having to shop for bulletproof clothing and cars.

What the paparazzi do is wrong, whether or not it's illegal, whether or not it gets anyone killed. There's no excuse for them. But that's not the end of the story, because they don't buy their own pictures. We buy them.

In an era where we seem to hold the virtues of the free market above all else, it's more important than ever to also be keenly aware of its vices. We all know that supply and demand has its seamy side. But as individuals, we don't seem to recognize the role we play. We're just the consumers, anonymous and detached. We sit on the sidelines and we watch.

It's difficult to recognize that our watching creates the market, that what each of us does really matters. The responsibility is so small that it seems insignificant. But it is not. If just one person moves a teaspoon of earth from one neighborhood to another, it makes no difference. But when a hundred million people do it, it creates a canyon, a floodplain, a wasteland. The same goes for sleazy media. Tiny, seemingly insignificant consumer actions—like watching a few minutes of a television show, or buying a tabloid at the supermarket—quickly add up to lucrative business. Each person who plunks down money or even a few moments of their precious attention is helping to create a heaving prurient beast.

There are two ways to control this beast. The first is legislation meant to protect us from ourselves. That's how Europe chooses to respond to the paparazzi, and this tragedy will no doubt serve to stiffen their resolve. Here in the United States, we choose the second, more difficult path. We trust the marketplace to correct itself. Ultimately, that means not the editors or the photographers, but us.

Again, I'm not arguing that we should absolve the goons who not only chased Dodi and Diana but also vulturously shot pictures of the wreckage that they may have helped create. But let us not forget that we are a part of their economy. We pay the people who pay them. In this way, we are complicit in the madness of celebrity. If we really want to kill the beast, all we have to do is stop feeding it with our gaze.

But is it possible to not look? Rubbernecking, it seems, is as human as kissing. When shocking or alluring things are put before us, we can't help but at least glance. Here's where I wholeheartedly endorse Brooke Shelby Biggs's exhortation to the media: stand up and do the honorable thing. Show some ethical backbone. Lead by example. When it comes to sleaze and celebrity journalism, there's a certain segment of moral responsibility that has to rest with the editors and producers. The market may beckon, but they are the ones who choose to publish these distorting, agitating images.

I also agree with Jon Katz that this isn't a subject where the "mainstream" media can credibly point any fingers. They're just as complicit as the tabloids are in mythmaking. ABC News, just as much as the *Star,* aggressively ballooned the image of Diana into that of a goddess, both before and after her death.

But ultimately, I believe, the issue comes back to the marketplace. Whether it's in the real or the virtual world, "hits" matter. Whatever we watch or read, wherever we web-surf, we help create a profitable market. We vote with our pocket change and our valuable attention. We are the ultimate commodity that all advertisers and for-profit journalists are after.

The information revolution is a marvel. It fuels (and celebrates) an empowering shift of control from giant bureaucracies to individuals. This is what Andrew Shapiro, a friend who is writing a fascinating book on the subject (for the Twentieth Century Fund), calls "the Control

Revolution." But with all the advantages of this diffusion of power and control, Shapiro points out that there is also a serious burden being passed on to the individual. "The shift from government to individual power means that we'll increasingly have to take on a variety of responsibilities ourselves," Shapiro says. "The problem is that the state does some things better, more efficiently. Unless we consciously relinquish power back, recognizing the benefits of representation, these responsibilities will sometimes turn into overly cumbersome burdens."

I think Shapiro is dead-on. Empowerment is a terrific thing, but it's easy to take it too far. What libertarians seem to want is an unrestricted marketplace that also adheres to the Golden Rule. That would be lovely, but I fear it's an inherent contradiction. When control becomes that diffuse, and consumers are somewhat detached from the collective power of their actions, the market can get a little ugly. If libertarians want to continue to argue their position, it behooves them to help the rest of us understand how the marketplace can correct its own character. I'm all ears.

Not Kissing but Telling Anyway

The Ethical Ramifications of Photoshop

Just a few weeks before the fatal car crash of Princess Diana and Dodi al-Fayed in Paris, the *Mirror,* a London tabloid, published a provocative picture of the glamorous new couple romancing on a boat, leaning in toward one another, apparently to kiss. It was all so revealing.

In fact, though, that kiss never happened. The picture had been digitally altered, Dodi's head rotated slightly to make it look as though a smooch were in the works.

The technical aspect of this manipulation will impress few, if any, *Hotwired* readers. Anyone who has spent five minutes fooling with Photoshop knows how simple this type of tampering can be. Photo-altering software may be the single best emblem of the immense new power conferred on humanity by the digital revolution: with just a little will and some patience, virtually anyone can do virtually anything to a photograph. Had the editors so desired, they easily could have shown Diana painting starbursts on Dodi's chest, with Boris Yeltsin standing right behind them, pinching Diana's butt.

But that's not the type of thing that most editors do with Photoshop. What they do is far more subtle and insidious. Take the case of Rebecca Sealfon, winner of this year's National Spelling Bee. Naturally, she was elated the moment she won. The Associated Press distributed a photograph of an exuberant teenager screaming for joy and waving her arms in the air. Hanging down in front of her ruffled white blouse was her large entrant placard. It read:

140
Daily News
New York, New York

This meant simply that Sealfon was entrant number 140, and that the *New York Daily News* was her sponsor for the event.

A curious thing happened, though, when the picture appeared

the next day in the *New York Post*, a *Daily News* competitor. The "140" was a lot bigger on the placard, and the phrase "Daily News" had vanished.

140
New York, New York

This excision is so petty and insubstantial, one might convincingly argue that it belongs in the Who Cares file. But I think it's quite significant as a symbol of what photographs are becoming in the wired world, and of the havoc that high-tech editors are already beginning to wreak on the institution of photojournalism.

Clearly, "photofiction," as some have come to call it, is potentially provocative as an art form (though there is plenty of room for skepticism here too—turning an ordinary photograph into a hallucinatory gallery of disassociated images does not automatically make it art). As a new journalistic tool, though, it is highly suspect. People look to photographs as quasi-objective representations of firsthand data, as a form of verification or proof. As soon as the essential integrity of a photo is undermined, so is the relationship between the news provider and the news consumer.

Obviously, there's no justification whatever for an editor digitally repositioning subjects in order to give a false impression that a kiss or slap or snub is taking place. But I would argue that the manipulation doesn't have to be nearly so flagrant in order to be unethical and damaging. When untidy or unappealing objects start getting cleaned up or removed, the essence of that photo also quickly disappears. The unspoken contract between the photographer and the viewer is broken. The photo is no longer any sort of glimpse of the scene. It is now much closer to a text or an illustration—an interpretation with selective facts, categorized in a particular way, with some details highlighted, many others simply obliterated. To relinquish the unique power of the photograph would be a grave mistake. We would soon miss it.

There is no such thing as true objectivity, of course, in photography or any other medium. By its very nature, a photograph is an incomplete and therefore slanted picture of reality—a stylized depiction that represents exactly what the photographer *wants* you to see, and no more. Each photograph is like a story, and we always have to remember that behind every story is a storyteller.

It's also worth recalling that conventional photo manipulations have been around as long as photographs. Cropping alone is a powerful tool, and there are plenty of basic darkroom techniques for removing or altering aspects of any photograph. Surrealist art photographers such as Jerry Uelsmann have captivated colleagues and collectors for decades by creatively embedding exotic foreign images into naturalistic landscapes.

Thankfully, though, Uelsmann doesn't try to pass his work off as reality. Nor is he under pressure to spike up sales on the newsstands. Photo editors' new digital sandbox threatens to cheapen journalism and even further undermine news consumers' confidence in the media. By making dramatic manipulations simple to effect and difficult to detect, photofiction threatens to exacerbate the climate of distrust.

Fortunately, there's an easy antidote, in the form of a full-disclosure proposal by former *New York Times Magazine* photo editor Fred Ritchin. Ritchin has developed a new icon, a tiny crossed-out camera lens, which he would like to see all photo editors affix to any published photographs with any digital alterations. It's a great idea, one that we would all do well to get behind.

Whether or not Ritchin's proposal catches on, there is likely to be one beneficial by-product of the digital poisoning of photojournalism. Sooner or later, the mass consumer audience will catch on to the manipulation, probably through a major celebrity scandal of some sort. When they do, they will permanently say goodbye to their image naïveté. A new variety of skepticism will flourish. Critical awareness of photojournalism's subjectivity will spread far and wide.

The very real danger, though, is that the skepticism will yield to a destructive cynicism. And if that happens, we will all be very sorry.

[Cover Story for *The Nation*, March 22, 1999]

Ph.D., Inc.

Ambitious partnering between the biotech industry and university science has had indisputable economic and health benefits. But is extreme profitability healthy for academia? Recent events and studies warn of unintended consequences.

The third most dispensed drug in the United States is a thyroid medication called Synthroid. Eight million Americans suffering from hypothyroidism take Synthroid every day, paying a premium for Knoll Pharmaceutical's top-selling brand name rather than buying the much-less-expensive generic alternative. Like most brand leaders, Knoll's enormous success with Synthroid is entirely dependent on its continuing ability to convince its users and the health care community that their drug is worth the extra cost. This they have done brilliantly for decades, despite any real proof of Synthroid's superiority.

In the late '80s, the company (then known as Boots Pharmaceutical) had good reason to believe that it was on the verge of obtaining such proof. A clinical pharmacist at the University of California at San Francisco named Betty Dong published a limited study that strongly suggested Synthroid would beat out its competitors in a blind, randomized trial. The company approached Dong, offering her the full $250,000 needed to pay for such a long and complex study.

Alas, the study backfired on the company. To the surprise of nearly everyone, including Betty Dong, the results suggested that Synthroid was no more or less effective than three much cheaper competitors. All four were what scientists call "bioequivalent."

But the company had a trump card. As the study's sponsor, it had not only been able to design the protocols of the drug trial; it also had exclusive access to the prepublished results of the study as well as final approval over whether the study could ever be made public at all. Not surprisingly, with the results so threatening to its marketing efforts, Knoll set out to thwart the study. In addition to delaying its publication by many years, effectively destroying the relevance of its data, the company also undermined the study's message by preemptively publishing the UCSF data in a different journal with a different, much friendlier, conclusion. Then they waged a massive PR campaign against the real study, "Bioequivalence of Generic and Brand-name Levothyroxine Products in the Treatment of Hypothyroidism," by Betty J. Dong et al., after it was finally published in the spring of 1997 in the eminent *Journal of the American Medical Association (JAMA)*.

A massive class action lawsuit followed the publication of Dong's *JAMA* report, alleging on behalf of all Synthroid users that Knoll had defrauded them of hundreds of millions of dollars in inflated cost. Knoll has offered to settle for a sum close to $100 million—what would be the largest cash settlement for a class action suit in history. And yet, even with such a fantastic price to pay, one can only conclude that in the end Knoll has benefited tremendously from its brash interference in the academic research process: A hundred million dollars is but a small fraction of the profits they made from Synthroid over the years that they were delaying or suppressing the study. And by their ability to taint Dong's study with enough controversy over the years, they were able to nullify any would-be effect. "Sales continue to grow very rapidly," Carter Eckert, Knoll's president, told me when I visited him at the company's rural New Jersey headquarters. "Our position has been validated."

Betty Dong's case, while extraordinary, is not isolated. In Toronto, liver specialist Nancy Olivieri was threatened with legal action by the Canadian drug giant Apotext if she published criticisms of its drug L1, concerns which had emerged from a clinical trial the company was sponsoring. In Providence, Brown University's director of occupational medicine, David Kern, was pressured both by a local company and by his own university not to publish his findings about a new lung disease breaking out at the company's plant. (Kern did publish his data and the disease, Flock Worker's Lung, was officially recognized by the U.S. Centers for Disease Control in September 1997.) In Winston-Salem, hypertension expert Curt Furberg (of Bowman Gray School of Medicine) and three colleagues resigned from a major Sandoz-funded study of calcium channel blockers rather than cave in to company pressure to spin negative results in a positive light. "I have seen people in industry asking for stranger and stranger things in private funding, as far as control is concerned," says Gregory Gardiner, Yale's Senior

Director of the Office of Cooperative Research. Indeed, these sensational cases may well be only the visible tip of a broader crisis in academic science. Over the last two decades, university-industry partnerships have become a ubiquitous feature of biotech research, and with this new closeness has come a raft of new concerns about whether the soul of academic science is being slowly eaten away. "We need to be vigilant," suggests Gardiner, "to make sure nothing is happening to university science."

The infusion of private capital is staggering. In 1997, U.S. companies spent an extraordinary $1.7 billion on university-based science and engineering research, a fivefold increase from 1977. More than 90 percent of life science companies now have some type of formal relationship with academic scientists, and 60 percent of those report that they have achieved new patents, products, and sales as a result. In the realm of university science, at least, that once-remote ivory tower now finds itself catty-corner to an office park—in many cases literally.

No one doubts this surge in university-industry alliances has produced enormous scientific progress, yielding important new drugs like the anti-HIV agent 3TC, a synthetic version of the anti-cancer drug Taxol, and the Haemophilus b conjugate children's vaccine for bacterial meningitis. University-industry alliances have also hatched many critical tests and medical technologies, prolonging and improving countless lives.

The new alliances have also generated a lot of profit. According to the Association of University Technology Managers, a boosterish pro-alliance trade group, corporate licensing of university inventions now accounts for $21 billion in annual revenue, which in turn supports 180,000 jobs. The arrangement has also become an important new revenue stream for academic institutions and for individual faculty: In 1993, the top ten universities alone received $170 million in product royalties. In the majority of campus technology transfer policies, the researchers making discoveries are entitled to a portion of that money. Sure enough, a 1993 survey of the fourteen leading U.S. biomedical journals by Tufts University's Sheldon Krimsky disclosed that 15 percent of lead authors had some significant financial interest in their published report. A similar survey in 1996 suggested the number was closer to one-third. "Companies say, 'Here's the design. Are you interested?'" explains Bowman Gray medical school's Curt

Furberg. "Being interested means a lot of funding for you and your institution. There's a lot of appeal in going along."

Unfortunately, the cost of economic success may often be the integrity of the science itself. What are we to make of a recent study published in *JAMA* suggesting that an astounding 43 percent of women and 31 percent of men suffer from "sexual dysfunction"—once we also discover that two of the study's authors served as paid consultants to Pfizer? (The relationships were not disclosed in *JAMA*). If individual researchers are profiting from their own research, considers University of Pennsylvania bioethicist Mildred Cho, "the outcome or direction of their work might be affected. They might, for instance, be tempted—consciously or unconsciously—to design studies that are more likely than not to have an outcome favorable to the product." Or they might be tempted to keep life-saving but potentially profitable information secret from the colleagues—now competitors—who could most readily build on the discovery. "There is little question that academic faculty have a very different and less critical attitude towards a specific company if they are getting a lot of money," insists Public Citizen's Sidney Wolfe. "It's not just research grants. A number of these people supplement their income by going around the country giving talks, funded by the drug industry. It adds a significant amount of money to their income. You don't bite the hand that feeds you." The obligation purchased with this money, Wolfe says, eats into "the freedom to teach the way you want to, to put drugs on the formulary, to do the research you want to do, to publish when you have results as opposed to when some company decides that it's OK. People don't have to sign restrictive agreements. You can modify people's behavior just by giving them money."

Such subtle and not-so-subtle perversions of science would be very difficult to detect but would have very real economic and health implications for American consumers. Adverse side effects might not be adequately reported; drugs and devices with head starts would maintain artificial leads—and premium prices. Scientists wouldn't always pursue drugs and tests that lack obvious short-term markets. Ultimately, private science would answer not to the public good, but to the same pressures that drive stocks up and down. "The reason we got the money [from Boots/Knoll] was that chances were that the results were going to be very positive," says Betty Dong, still an important researcher at UCSF. "I've changed my mind about that. I don't think that's a very good reason to do research."

Whatever the drawbacks of the privatization of research, logic would dictate that they are already pervasive. "Some of the collaborations I find strange," says Allen Sinisgalli, Princeton's associate provost. "If you're involved in sponsored research and you're working on one floor and the corporation is on the other floor, it's hard to believe that the stairwell somehow acts a membrane that will prevent conflicts of interest." While private investment amounts to just 12 percent of the total annual budget for academic life science, that number nevertheless signals a radical shift in the funding of American science—a shift which is causing considerable concern among a small group of academic ethicists. "An entrepreneurial atmosphere has begun to alter the ethos of science," warns Sheldon Krimsky. "Norms of behavior within the academic community are being modified to accommodate closer corporate ties."

This is not to say that medical research is rife with corruption. But there are unmistakable warning signs. One recent study, for example, revealed that among published studies of new drug therapies, 98 percent of those financially supported by the pharmaceutical industry commented favorably on the new drug—in contrast to 79 percent of studies with no industry support. Ninety-eight percent: either industry-supported studies are consistently and miraculously beating all the odds, or a raft of unfavorable results is somehow not getting published. "This is the biggest ethical issue facing biomedical research now and into the twenty-first century," says Mildred Cho. "It's something that's sneaking up on us now, and shouldn't be."

If you're ever curious to see what an ethicist looks like trying to crawl out of his or her own skin, offer to spring for lunch. This is the level of consternation I have unintentionally created as I meet with Drummond Rennie in San Francisco. "I'm sorry, I can't. I just can't let you do that—but please let me explain why," Rennie, the West Coast/deputy editor of *JAMA*, pleads in his plaintive Winchester-Cambridge accent as I try to pay for our mayonnaisey sandwiches just downstairs from his office. Jerking out his black leather billfold, Rennie explains his longtime, iron-clad rule of refusing all offers of free food, travel, lodging—indeed, perks of any kind—from anyone other than his employer. Polite apologies are exchanged, accepted. No harm done. Our mutual autonomy intact, we head back upstairs. As I set up my tape recorder, Rennie, who over the years has slowly fashioned himself into the conscience not only of *JAMA* but more generally of scientific publishing, opens his file drawer and begins to excavate the Synthroid files.

A junior associate, Veronica Yank, lends a hand. There isn't much glory in the business of ethical scrutiny, and certainly not much money; it's not the type of job that filters into the daydreams of ambitious children or that charming recruiters wax eloquent about over seared tuna to recent Phi Beta Kappa graduates. So here at the Institute for Health Policy Studies—a think tank affiliated with UCSF's prestigious medical school, where, on top of his *JAMA* duties, he teaches—Rennie has also made an effort to mentor other like-minded scientists. While most of the world's researchers investigate matters of efficacy, morbidity, and so on, this small cadre—Yank, Cho, and Rennie protégé Lisa Bero (herself now a leading force in the field)—join Krimsky and Harvard's David Blumenthal in examining the integrity of that research. It's nothing like a police squad, though, because most of the flaws and compromises they discover are not even apparent to the researchers. Due to corporate influence, says Rennie, "there is distortion that causes publication bias in little ways, and scientists just don't understand that they have been influenced. There's influence everywhere, on people who would steadfastly deny it. You and I think we are not influenced, but Veronica looking at us from above can prove that we are."

Like most of his ethics colleagues, Rennie, 61, did not leap at but slowly gravitated to the field. Trained in nephrology—the study of kidneys—at the University of London and Johns Hopkins, he eventually managed to combine his vocational specialty with his avocational passion—high-altitude climbing—to become an expert on altitude sickness. Throughout the 1960s and '70s, in dozens of expeditions in the Andes, the Himalayas, the Alps, the Yukon, and Alaska, Rennie documented the physiological effects of low-oxygen environments. A 1981 hip injury on Mount McKinley squelched that intense phase of his life, but he took away from his mountain years a profound lesson in morality. "Really serious climbing teaches you a lot about integrity," he says. "It's so basic—do you abandon someone or not when you think you're going to die? Do you cut the rope? Do you make an effort to get food up to those people? There are a lot of very stark things that climbing teaches which I've found very painful to learn, because I haven't always made the right choices."

In 1977, Rennie went to work for Arnold "Bud" Relman at the *New England Journal of Medicine*. In Relman, Rennie found a mentor for what would become the next distinguished phase of his career. At first, the education was simply in the art of scientific editing. Interest in the integrity of scientific literature came later, and was driven by a series of unfortunate events. "I came into this role very slowly," he says. "It took a long time for me to even accept that there was such a thing as scientific misconduct."

His terrifying introduction to the subject came in 1979 in the form of a letter to the *New England Journal of Medicine* containing incontrovertible proof that two Yale researchers, Vijay Soman and Philip Felig, had committed plagiarism. Not long after that, a well-respected Harvard researcher, John Darsee, was caught faking a date on an electrocardiogram. "When I heard that there was a problem with Darsee," says Rennie, "I rushed to the *Journal*. We had just published this amazing article by him. I looked at it again and said to myself, 'Oh, we're all right. He's got a co-author and he thanked three other authors at the end of the article.' Well, it was later shown that every single piece of data in that article was invented. He even invented the doctors at the end."

The Synthroid case is Rennie's latest fascination because, he says, it so clearly illustrates the starkly differing agendas of industry and the academy. "This was a good study," he says. "The best study that had been published on the subject. They went to extraordinary efforts to discredit it, and by extraordinary I mean that there were accusations that can ruin a scientist's career."

Indeed, when the research that Boots/Knoll had funded produced results that could potentially cost them billions, Knoll accused Dong not only of sloppy research, but also of serious ethical violations (none of which have been substantiated). Those accusations continue to this day. "We thought we had contracted with a qualified researcher," Carter Eckert told me during my visit to Knoll. "She didn't follow the protocol. Her methods were flawed. She drew erroneous conclusions and she didn't provide all the information on what she discovered."

While there does seem to be an honest scientific disagreement at the heart of the controversy, it's just as clear that the company exploited that difference well beyond propriety. "What Boots tried to do," says Leslie Benet, chairman of pharmaceutical chemistry at UCSF and one of the leading bioequivalency experts in the United States, "was to come in and create confusion as best they could—anything to delay or prevent the publication of this study. So they raised a lot of issues. They had a catalog of a hundred and something issues. The great majority of it was grandstanding, what we call 'data-scrubbing'—trying to find something to cause a problem."

Knoll also used its near-omnipotence in the thyroid community to keep the study under wraps, Rennie says. Perhaps the most vivid illustration of this came when the American Thyroid Association considered a resolution urging the company to allow the study to be published. "That vote was on an absolute no-brainer, which was, 'Should we, as the Thyroid Association, write to the manufacturer and say, Please publish this paper.' I can't think of any easier question. It's a matter of basic academic freedom. And it was turned down. That is most extraordinary." One inescapable conclusion is that the defeat had something to do with the fact that Knoll provides more than 60 percent of the American Thyroid Association's funding. Indeed, Rennie claims that three people present for the fateful vote later told him that as they considered the proposition, one member openly remarked that "we mustn't kill the golden goose."

"Universities exist to do research, and research exists to benefit mankind," Rennie says. "Companies have an additional and different agenda—making profit. Though they may be experts and though you may have read papers by them and so on, their strings are pulled by the marketers. And that's forgotten by academics."

Weeks later, in a follow-up phone conversation, I ask Rennie if the Dong-Synthroid affair is the worst case of private abuse of public research that he has ever seen. He laughs. "David, I've got a house full of files with important cases of abuse. This is just one example. There are many others. Extreme examples like faking whole papers draw attention, but trimming, skewing, using the wrong analysis, or using the more favorable analysis, or just muddling a little bit is certainly much more common and a far, far bigger problem."

For precisely fifty years, the U.S. government has funded, on our behalf, a stunning volume of academic scientific research, mostly through the umbrella bureaucracy of the National Institutes of Health. The expenditures have also been spectacular in their consistency. In sharp contrast to almost all other federal spending on research and development, spending on academic science has steadily increased through deficits, recessions, wars, and even our recent political devolution. The latter half of the twentieth century of American history might ultimately be as well known for its commitment to basic scientific research as for any other endeavor.

As the United States began to rebuild its economy after World War II, a conviction emerged among the elite that the nation's future success would depend largely on scientific progress. The spur came from the legendary Vannevar Bush, director of the wartime Office of Scientific Research and Development and overseer of the Manhattan Project. In July 1945, Bush submitted to President Truman a report entitled "Science—The Endless Frontier," which pleaded with Truman to make science a permanent national priority. "Without scientific progress," Bush wrote, "no amount of achievement in other directions can insure our health, prosperity, and security as a nation in the modern world."

Bush's expectation of science's importance to society has of course proven entirely correct. America's enthusiastic public support for research has helped make it the world's undisputed leader in public health. Part of that success is due to the fact that science was not only well funded for so long, but also had the independence to pursue its own ends. "Investigators did not have to prove the short-term applicability of their work," explains Harvard's David Blumenthal, "because they did not have to rely on sponsors, such as industry, with short-term orientations."

The implicit pact between scientists and legislators that allowed for such a long leash was that research dollars would, eventually, help treat and cure disease, something any constituency could appreciate. In part because the economy was performing so well in other areas, there was no particular expectation of economic benefits from this federal largesse for several decades. American industry was too busy manufacturing to bother with discovery. Throughout the 1950s and '60s, private industry generated less than 4 percent of all university research funding. This "certainly did not prevent the transfer of useful technologies from universities to biomedical industries," remarks

Blumenthal. "But it did result in less direct interaction between academic scientists and industrial organizations."

In the late 1970s, as the American economy faltered and strong foreign competition emerged from Japan and western Europe, the institutional separation between academia and industry came under critical scrutiny as both industry and government began to view academic science as an untapped economic resource. Many potentially lucrative discoveries, it was thought, were foundering in the laboratory. In 1980, Congress passed the Bayh-Dole Act, which allowed researchers and universities to patent discoveries from federally funded research. With such legal protection, entrepreneurs would be able to take the development risks necessary to bring discoveries to market. Since almost everything on campus depends on Washington funding, at least in part, Bayh-Dole effectively lifted a ban on campus entrepreneurship, thus allowing academic scientists to take an active role in the private applications of their research.

The Federal Technology Transfer Acts of 1986 and 1989 strengthened market incentives even further, allowing researchers, for example, to keep proprietary information secret. This suite of legislation reflected an increasingly popular notion that government research was useful mainly as an economic seed. "There are also times when a field of research no longer needs the Government as nursemaid," the *New York Times* editorialized in 1985. "The rich flow of venture capital into biotechnology means the Government need no longer support that element of biomedical research so heavily." Between these lines, one can see the rebirth of a familiar laissez-faire refrain: what's good for Pfizer is good for everyone.

That sentiment would probably sound about right to Knoll Pharmaceutical president Carter Eckert. "The whole concept of this conflict—it ain't there," he said. "Not in the pharmaceutical business. The stakes are too high. It's absolutely insane to take the position that a pharmaceutical company is going to win by not pursuing the truth. Ultimately, the patients have to use the drug." In Eckert's view, then, the marketplace is the ultimate consumer watchdog. After all, he says, no one's going to make much money selling something that doesn't work.

That's true enough. On the other hand, the profit motive might encourage a company to suppress or distort research trumping competing products—or, for that matter, simply to keep some data secret. A 1997 survey by David Blumenthal revealed that, among companies that sponsor academic research, 58 percent require their investigators to withhold results for more than six months—far longer than the two months the NIH considers reasonable. In that same survey, a third of the academic respondents said they had been denied access to research results of other university scientists.

Ultimately, such secrecy costs not just dollars but also lives: Renowned NIH cancer researcher Stephen Rosenberg reports that he has, on several occasions, been unable to obtain important data and lab materials because he would not agree to strict proprietary rules of secrecy. When anything undermines the open sharing of all research data, laments Blumenthal, "researchers unknowingly build on something less than the total accumulation of scientific knowledge." Ineffective or even dangerous drugs are not revealed as such at the earliest possible moment; avenues of research already known to be fruitless by some are needlessly pursued by others, wasting money and time and ultimately hindering scientific progress.

The walls in Rennie's small office are lined with stark photographs of peaks, glaciers, and very cold people. "One of the great things about being a climber," Rennie says with a gesture to one wall, "is that you keep falling off things, and getting frozen. You end up in hospitals. You become a patient." He laughs. "It's my job, and Blumenthal's and Krimsky's and Bero's, to look at research from the patient's point of view, to ask, 'Can I trust this?' You can talk about caveat emptor, buyer beware, but patients are emptors that can't caveat because they don't know how. When you are a patient, it's not like buying a Toyota. Patients don't know how to choose their own anesthetic."

Such profoundly important medical decisions are made by hospital boards based on the best scientific research available. The problem is, argues Rennie, that as universities continue to let industry money dilute their nonprofit, nonpartisan character, they do so at the risk of frittering away public confidence. "The bottom line for universities that they haven't fully understood," he says, "is that in the end, public universities have to rely on public support. If the public perceives a university as a place where scientists become millionaires and where companies are in control, they'll lose public support, and that will be catastrophic for them, and for the public at large. People will say, 'Well, he's got a bigger house than I have, and a better car, and I don't seem to be getting any of the action at all. Why should I support or do anything to help those jerks? They're just a rich business concern.' Universities have to have credibility and be above the fray."

Princeton's Sinisgalli agrees. "Universities are having difficulty all the way along the line," he says. "We cannot allow ourselves to blur our role. It's not only a matter of conflict of interest, but also of conflict of commitment and time." Though industry-sponsored research on his campus has risen sixfold in recent years as a portion of total research dollars, it's only at about half the national average. Further, Princeton retains what may be the strictest industry-sponsorship policies in the country: no developmental research; no testing; no ownership stake allowed in any company sponsoring campus research. "For a while, a lot of people thought we were a little behind the curve," says Sinisgalli. "Now, I think some people are looking at our cautiousness and saying, 'Maybe they were right.' They are rethinking it because there are so many conflicts."

One obvious move that bioethicists would like to see is a lot more public disclosure. While most of the top research institutions have disclosure guidelines in place, many could be more stringent. Conferences and journals have also been edging toward more disclosure, but many refuse to budge. *Nature* magazine, for example, insisted in an editorial last year that the 1996 report by Sheldon Krimsky revealing that a third of authors surveyed had a financial interest in the research "makes no claim that the undeclared interests led to any fraud, deception, or bias in presentation, and until there is evidence that there are serious risks of such malpractice, this journal will persist in its stubborn belief that research as we publish it is indeed research, not business."

Nature's position of shielding conflicts of interest from public view is ridiculous on its face and, in an era of so many financial entanglements, a threat to the integrity of science. The starkness of the problem was revealed earlier last year in a *New England Journal of Medicine* survey of authors who had published studies on calcium channel blockers, a controversial class of drugs purported to decrease the risk of heart attacks. "The medical profession has failed to develop and enforce strict guidelines for disclosing conflict of interest," the *NEJM* survey concluded. How did they arrive at such a blunt determination? It turned out that while just 3 percent of the calcium channel authors surveyed had publicly disclosed potential conflicts of interest, the percentage of those who should have—that is, the percentage of those who publicly favored the drug and had a financial relationship with the manufacturers—was somewhat higher: 96.

The World According to You

The Problem with Personalized News

Imagine this dream scenario: you wake up in the morning, walk outside in your pajamas to get the paper, sit down with your golden toasted everything-bagel and your first cup of double-half-caf-cappuccino-no-foam-with-a-pinch-of-cinnamon, and you open up the paper to take in the news.

I know—so far, that's just a Seattle-esque kind of morning. Here's the surreal part: the paper has your name at the top. If your name is Eric Berlow, it's called *The Eric Berlow Gazette*. Then you notice that every article in this morning's paper is directly relevant to your life. The lead story is about a rare plant species that you happen to be studying. The story just below that has a quote from your domineering-but-influential boss. The story below that is about Buffalo, New York, your hometown.

You flip to the Sports section. It contains nothing but articles about your favorite athletes and teams. There isn't an irrelevant score or picture in the whole section. Same with the business page—it features only stories about companies that you have worked for and invested in. It's as if the editor of the paper is an obsessed fan of yours. Instead of stalking you day and night, she has found out everything there is to know about you and tailored the news to your exact tastes.

But this isn't *Fatal Attraction Goes to the Newsroom*. It's the future of news—and not just the future—but also the present, as you will see when you check out the customizable Internet news sites "Crayon" (CReAte Your Own Newspaper), "My Yahoo," and Infoseek's "your news" news center. Interactive software known as "smart agents" can now selectively pick news reports based strictly on a set of keywords from you.

The result is a constantly updated electronic newspaper on your computer screen that has no irrelevant material. No articles about Bosnia, if you're bored of that subject. No articles about Newt Gingrich, if you're sick and tired of reading about him. No art films, if that's not your thing. The magic of the Information Age is that you get to spend as much time as you want in your own niche.

Have you caught on to the problem yet? It's that niche media taken to this extreme is a very dangerous thing. Sure, it's a lifestyle booster. You can follow stock-car racing details or whale-watching reports or soccer scores all day long.

But the death of general interest media comes at a serious cost to society. When technology allows us to skip over stories about other people's concerns, communities evaporate.

One of the great ironies of the Net is that as it plugs us into the entire universe of information, it also encourages isolation. You can spend all breakfast reading your customized newspaper. But what are you going to talk about in the carpool?

V.

the world and redmond, washington

Thoughts on Microsoft

[Written for, but not published on, *MSN*, October 1996]

Deep Pockets

The Problem with a Free Microsoft Browser

The most successful software outfit on the planet is suddenly having a fire sale. Why?

Microsoft, the company that brought you Word (price: $300 at Egghead Software), Excel (also $300), and Windows 95 ($189), among other popular programs, is offering its latest cutting-edge Internet software for a price many web surfers might find difficult to resist: $0. This grand giveaway is the mother of all *free stuff!* bonanzas on the Net, and begs to be scrutinized with equal intensity.

Netscape, Microsoft's primary competitor in the Internet browser business, sells versions of its Navigator for $49 to $86. One might expect a late-coming competitor like Microsoft to aggressively undercut that price by 10 to 20 percent. Instead, Microsoft is giving away as many copies as possible, and investing enough programming resources into free upgrades to turn them out as often as every six months.

It's as if McDonald's up and announced that for the foreseeable future, bacon double cheeseburgers will be free to anyone who can make it to the counter and ask nicely. Oh, and McDonald's will be spending millions of R&D money figuring out how to make this free sandwich taste even better.

How on earth is Microsoft going to earn a profit by giving its costly products away? Whatever the plan, it must be impressive to spreadsheet types, because it has inspired a surge in Microsoft's stock price (up 75 percent from its lowest price in the last twelve months)—while most other Internet stocks (including Netscape's) have come a-tumblin' down down down.

The answer is *volume*. Microsoft plans to make a lot of money in the long term by bleeding money profusely in the short term. Microsoft's strategy is a variant of what is sometimes called predatory pricing.

Predatory pricing is a game only large, cash-rich businesses can play, whereby they wield their deep pockets like box cutters against smaller competitors by temporarily dropping their prices so far below those of their competitor that neither company could turn any profit at all.

Think of Wal-Mart, Barnes & Noble, Citibank. If you have seen any of these gorillas stomp into your neighborhood and threaten a local mom & pop operation with spectacular deals (in an old neighborhood a few years back, Citibank actually paid me $50 for each account I set up), you know all about predatory pricing. These are companies so rich, they can afford to sacrifice short-term profit in an aim to gain market share.

The ultimate aim in normal predatory pricing schemes is to gain 100 percent market share by driving the smaller competitors out of business. When Citibank is the only guy left standing, that's when the prices start to creep up again.

With Microsoft, it's a lot more complicated than that. For one thing, Microsoft has said up-front that all future versions of Internet Explorer will be free, and I think we can take Bill Gates on his word about that. Rather, what Apple, Oracle, Netscape, Sun Microsystems, and the U.S. Justice Department (not to mention thousands of savvy web surfers) are really worried about is a Microsoft-dominated Internet.

When and if Microsoft's Internet Explorer becomes *the* standard browsing software for the Internet in the same way that Windows software has become the industry standard operating software for PCs, the Net could become a very different place, with much less software innovation and an almost unimaginable stream of power and money flowing into Microsoft coffers. Contrary to the hope of some Net entrepreneurs that some day soon the majority of Net users could be using "applets" to bypass Windows altogether, the interdependence of Windows-run PCs and an IE-dominated Internet could make Microsoft *the* information powerhouse well into the next century. To consider the drawbacks of such control, one need only recall how expensive and cumbersome long-distance calling was when AT&T controlled all the levers.

Free stuff: it sometimes helps the consumer in the short run, but in the long run it never comes for free. Microsoft's massive giveaway is their way of saying "Eat now, pay later—when we're the only restaurant in town."

Hating Gates

The Culture of Microsoft Bashing

It's kind of funny that Bill Gates has embraced the World Wide Web with so much enthusiasm and investment capital lately, because the Web sure doesn't seem to like him much. Try an AltaVista search for "Microsoft sucks" and you'll see what I mean. In cyberspace, Gates is repeatedly shot at, poked in the face with darts, and revealed to be the devil (there's lots of proof!). Offline, meanwhile, Gates's list of antagonists seems to be mushrooming almost as fast as his net worth, with vocal detractors in every branch of the federal government, a significant number of state attorney general's offices, the national media, brand-name universities, and leading consumer action groups—all supported by a grassroots chorus of software engineers, web professionals, corporate systems managers, and disgruntled customers. Competitors and consumers vilify him and his company with smugness and a casual ferocity. "There is a definite subcurrent of dissatisfaction and real animosity towards Microsoft," says Paul Gillin, editor in chief of *Computerworld.* "Whenever I write a column that is critical of Microsoft, invariably, a half-dozen 'attaboy letters will come out of the woodwork—'Way to go,' 'Stick it to 'em,' 'Evil empire,' and 'They suck.'" Gillin's published praise for Microsoft draws the same sentiments. "I get letters saying, 'You're just sucking up,' 'You're in Bill Gates's back pocket,' or 'You suck.'" These acid notes, Gillin says, do not seem to come from a short list of recycled names. "It's a wide and diverse group." Microsoft-bashing has become so common in the Bay Area, says writer Po Bronson, "it's like talking about the weather in Minnesota. I literally have conversations about Microsoft with everybody, every day, all the time. It is omnipresent."

But to what end? Is there any validity or seriousness of purpose behind the incessant Darth Vader imputations, or is Microsoft-bashing just another way of pretending, as we all did with the O.J. trial for a while, that we still have a common culture? Worse yet, are the growing number of Gates-haters simply pawns of high-octane competitors like Lotus, Oracle, Netscape, and Sun, for whom Microsoft-hating is an important part of doing business? "If you want your company to get some attention," complains Microsoft spokesman Greg Shaw, "you say, 'Hmmm, how might I get my company covered? I'll think I'll come down on Bill Gates.'"

He's dead right, of course, and no one has done more to whip up the hostility than Netscape, Microsoft's archrival in the web browser business. Marc Andreeson publicly compares Microsoft to the Mafia, boasting that his company refused what was supposed to be Microsoft's *unrefusable* offer to buy them out. "No horse's head in the bed yet," Andreeson says. He also characterizes the current Netscape-Microsoft browser contest as Bambi vs. Godzilla, portraying his company as not only the underdog, but also as the ethically pure protagonist. Andreeson knows that Americans can't stand to see bullies win in the end.

Condemning Gates not only helps companies gain the visibility and public admiration that they crave; it also serves as ideal internal propaganda. Software is a quixotic and ruthless business. Vast fortunes are made and lost these days in very short order, and hardworking employees of ambitious companies easily slip into a bunker mentality. For those tens of thousands of people working off not much more than dark-roasted coffee fumes and stock options, Gates is not just a formidable competitor. He is also the ideal motivational device, a marionette of hate tugged by CEOs like Oracle's Larry Ellison, Sun's Scott McNeally, and Lotus's Jeffrey Papows. (Papows and McNeally, Papows has said, are "co-captains of the I-hate-Bill-Gates fan club. We just couldn't decide which of us hates him more.") Ellison rallied his troops last year by displaying a giant computer-generated image of Gates giving Oracle employees the finger. Many thousands of industry laborers hate Microsoft mostly because they are trained to. But that doesn't mean the rest of us should go along.

Other harsh critics obsess about what they insist is the insulting mediocrity of the company's software. (Joke précis: Bill Gates dies and gets to choose between Heaven and Hell. On his tour of Hell, it looks like a beach party, in contrast with Heaven's park bench serenity. After he chooses Hell, though, it turns out to be a torturous, skin-flaying pit of despair. Gates asks St. Peter, "What gives? What happened to the Hell you showed me before?" St. Peter looks down—from his Macintosh—and says, "Oh, that was just the demo.") MS "crapware," as some call it, is said to be inelegant and buggy. "I hate Microsoft because I am frequently put in a position of solving problems that would not have come up if my customer had bought software from another vendor," one information systems manager says. Another software professional (both insist on anonymity for reasons for job security) echoes this complaint, denouncing "their dominance of the software industry with crap." But it's nothing personal, he adds. "I would probably hate anyone who dominates the industry with the use of bad software."

Hundreds of web pages have sprung up to protest Microsoft's allegedly inferior products. On the Net, there are endless how-many-Microsofties-does-it-take-to-screw-in-a-lightbulb quips, Gates-bought-*what?* spoofs, and I-hate-Bill-becauses. There is also a deluge of adolescent puns (Microsnot, Microshaft, Microsuck, etc.), a Usenet conference called "alt.destroy.microsoft," and enough gratuitous violence to fill out a Tarantino script ("Kill Bill Gates" appears twice as often as "Kill Bill Clinton"). An alien logging on from his own planet might be curious to know whether Gates had killed more people than Adolf Hitler, or slightly fewer.

"It started when I saw my dad using Windows and it crashed every five minutes," says Chris Mutter, the twenty-four-year-old Austrian creator of what he claims was the very first anti-Microsoft "Hate Page": www.enemy.org, which went online in 1994. "I was just angry because here was a company who is the leader in the PC software market and ships its products with that many bugs and limitations." Enemy.org, a member of something called the International Anti-MS Network, features many of the classics in the hate-Bill genre—the "Internet Exploder" and "WinBlows" parody icons, the depiction of Gates with horns and glowing red eyes, the gun to Gates's exploding head, and so on, much of it clearly the work of adolescent lampooners who tend not to fully consider the implications of what they're saying, but who are nonetheless reacting instinctively to a corporate behemoth that appears to put profits first, consumers second, and technological excellence last. "YOU have been part of a force that has done everything humanly possible to ensure that using a computer . . . is a living hell for any person without a legal education," writes enemy.org contributor Rune Jacobsen to any MS employees who might happen to be visiting the site. "You therefore have to accept that you are a subject of hate from computer users all over the world, and this is our only way to get back at you."

If their software is so inferior and they treat their customers that badly, though, how does Microsoft prevail in the free market? The widely accepted explanation for Microsoft's astounding success simply reinforces the antipathy: First, Microsoft was able to establish MS-DOS and subsequently Windows as the standard PC operating system by exacting a royalty for every PC sold regardless of whether its operating system was installed. Then the company leveraged its ubiquity and deep pockets to push products like Microsoft Office, Encarta, and Internet Explorer.

It does seem pretty clear that Microsoft used anti-competitive tactics to secure its market position and sell a lot of software that wouldn't necessarily have sold that well on merit alone. The irony, though, is that as the "crapware" web sites proliferate, Microsoft is now using its wealth to dramatically improve its products. "This time," Apple co-founder Steve Jobs told *Fortune* last year, "Microsoft has the technology to compete on quality." Far from succumbing to the pride of success and indolence that can come with immense wealth (thousands of current and former Microsoft employees are stock-options millionaires), the company is maintaining its hunger for future success, plowing an extraordinary amount of resources into increasing the quality of its software. In many cases, Microsoft is funding several separate internal software teams competing with one another to come up with the best product.

If MS-bashers aren't just stooges of competitive propaganda, then, they begin to look like compulsive grumblers—malcontents who prefer to continuously kvetch about the lousy weather, to the point where they don't even notice that the sun is coming out. In the acrid digital space of the most vociferous Microsoft haters, truth and innuendo are intertwined to form a preposterous case against the company and its leader. "This company has executed its game plan so perfectly," says *Computerworld*'s Gillin. "But [the critics] won't recognize the brilliance in the business plan, so they think there must be some evil there supporting it."

From this angle, Microsoft comes off as the prom queen who, simply by virtue of her sheer good looks, spurs a steady undercurrent of resentment. "Microsoft is in a bind," says *Boston Globe* technology columnist Simson Garfinkel. "If they put out bad software, people criticize them for putting out bad software, and if they put out good software, people criticize them for dominating the industry."

If much of the vituperation seems either stale or contrived—or, in the case of Gates-basher-come-lately Orrin Hatch, simply a matter of good constituent service (Novell, another major competitor, is based in Utah)—there is also something authentic and compelling about the resentment. To begin with, some of the competitors' claims are, in addition to being self-serving, credible. When Gary Reback, the well-known Silicon Valley attorney who represents a number of Microsoft's competitors, passes on the popular gibe that "theirs is a praying mantis business model; they have sex with you and then they eat you," it is partly a sincere reflection of the bizarre state of the marketplace. "The basic model in the industry today is to be bought by Microsoft or to go out of business," observes Andrew Shapiro, a fellow at Harvard Law School's Berkman Center for Internet and Society. "Isn't that amazing? There's very little hope" of independent success. Software entrepreneurs really are in the position, in other words, of having to answer to Microsoft in much the same way that a bookie has to answer to the regional Mafia don.

And this overwhelming dominance is not due solely to the fact that, as Microsoft lackeys are fond of asserting, Bill Gates is always the smartest person in the room, nor to the fact that power and wealth naturally begets more power and wealth. The Justice Department's original anti-trust investigation and 1994 consent decree settlement confirmed that Microsoft's practices had been anti-competitive, and the department has recently accused the company of renewed deception. "Microsoft seeks to rewrite [its own] history," the department charged, "to disavow everything it has told millions of consumers." Echoing this charge, serious critics soberly contend that, while malevolence is clearly not an explicit objective of Microsoft, it is an integral part of the company's modus operandi. Microsoft's brilliance, they argue, is coated with a layer of duplicity that gives it an unfair advantage. "I'm not one of those who think Bill Gates is the devil," offers *InfoWorld* columnist and well-established critic Nicholas Petreley. "I simply suspect that if Microsoft ever met up with the devil, it wouldn't need an interpreter. They lie as if it's their native language. There's always a certain amount of deception in every company, but it's rarely as habitual or pathological as it is with Microsoft."

One apparent tactic which Petreley, Reback, and others object to is "vaporware," the strategy of quelling interest in a competitor's product through the use of tantalizing press releases. "In their typical vaporware act," says Audrie Krause, editor of the watchdog newsletter *The Microsoft Monitor*, "they say, 'We have this product that will soon be ready.'" This persuades many prospective purchasers to put on the brakes, she says. "It makes people say, 'Well I guess we'll wait and see.' They've done this repeatedly over the years, and sometimes they don't even ever bring out the product. But they kill the market for another product by announcing way ahead of time that they're coming out with something competitive."

Microsoft has also been accused of patent infringement; in one case, a jury awarded $120 million to Stac Electronics. The fallout of suspicion from incidents like this is compounded by occasional (Petreley alleges "constant") disingenuous comments from Gates and his lieutenants. "In a field like ours," Gates told NBC a few years ago, "there isn't much in the way of power." That's a little bit like Paul McCartney saying there isn't very much money to be made in the music business. In a similar reality-defying assertion earlier this year, Gates denied flatly in front of a group of newspaper editors that *Sidewalk*, Microsoft's new online network of city guides, was hiring established journalists; the evidence was clearly to the contrary. Petreley also cites a *Wall Street Journal* column in which Gates argued that if competitors can include such operating system functions as printing and application-launching in their web browsers, then it's fair for Microsoft to incorporate browser functions in their operating system. "That implies that the browser is competing with the OS," protests Petreley. "It is clearly exploiting the public's lack of technical knowledge."

"People don't hate Bill for his success," says an executive in a competing company. "They hate him for his fundamental dishonesty. He's not an inventor, he's an acquisitor."

The spate of Gates's recent acquisitions, in fact, seems to provoke another contingent of Microsoft detractors, one which fears not its stature but its breadth. "It goes beyond high-tech companies," says Bob

Ingle, Knight-Ridder's vice president for new media. "I think a fair chunk of corporate America is terrified of Microsoft, and they want an alternative." In the last dozen years, Gates and Microsoft have purchased a handful of promising software outfits, hired thousands of star programmers and researchers, co-founded a new cable network (MSNBC), snapped up the digital rights to the Bettman Archive of still images, and invested heavily in cable TV (Comcast), satellites (Teledesic), network computing (Web-TV), and other Internet-related resources. "They are obviously going after the means to control all ways of accessing the Internet," says *Microsoft Monitor*'s Krause. She notes a recent *Wall Street Journal* article quoting a top Microsoft executive on the company's explicit goal to get a "vig," or small percentage, of every Internet transaction using Microsoft software. "That is a term that comes straight out of organized crime," says Krause.

Microsoft's unrelenting ferocity not only draws the interest of consumer activists such as Ralph Nader. It also riles ordinary consumers like Mitch Stone, creator of the "Boycott Microsoft" web site, who stresses his lack of commercial interest in the issue. "My relationship to the industry," he says, "is that I use a computer." Stone says that he doesn't hate Microsoft personally, but is greatly offended by its corporate behavior. "To me, there is a difference between competition and what they do. In August 1996, Microsoft began aggressively distributing Explorer 3.0 for free. That seemed unfair to me, a pretty deliberate effort to destroy a much smaller competitor. As a consumer, I couldn't see how that benefited me any, or anyone else either. There is such a thing as being a good corporate citizen, and deliberate efforts to remove competitors from the marketplace—that's an ethical violation." (As a matter of fact, Steve Ballmer, Microsoft's vice president of sales, told *Fortune* in January 1997: "We're giving away a pretty good browser as part of the operating system. How long can they survive selling it?") Ethics aside, the prospect of any one company dominating what is commonly touted as an inherently decentralized medium understandably rankles anyone who believes in the virtue of the Internet.

What about the rest of us? Why have I, for example, casually bashed Microsoft in conversation, nonchalantly referring to the software-media giant as the "evil empire" plenty of times, before and after I cashed my Microsoft checks (for some online commentary I wrote for the Microsoft Network)? Why does the acrimony feel as ubiquitous in New York City as Po Bronson says it is in California?

One spur is Gates's weedy wealth. When he was worth just three or four billion dollars, it was heady, the unlikely triumph of a computer geek. Forty billion, though, invokes in many of us a vague sense of unease, compounded by the fact that it comes from the sales of hundreds of millions of products that, stacked together, wouldn't stretch to the end of your driveway, or even to the end of your hand. It's software, a batch of machine code. Microsoft is the second most capitalized company on the planet, and the only corporate colossus in history whose entire product line could be vaporized with a giant magnet.

The more powerful reason is techno-angst. The current phase of the information revolution has been a psychic whirlwind, for good and for ill. Software—particularly Microsoft software—has become so vital in our everyday lives, such an integral part of our culture, it is almost impossible to imagine life without it. (If forced to give up either your personal computer or one finger for the rest of your life, which would you choose? One in three would lose the digit, according to Philip Nicholson, one expert on "technostress." In my own informal surveying, the large number of people who actually ponder this question as a genuine dilemma is what impresses even more.) The remarkable velocity of information and increased demand on a consumer's attention can also produce significant stress and distraction. Our emerging "attention economy," whereby profits are determined by how much of a consumer's attention a company is able to capture, inevitably yields a noisier, more vulgar society.

In venting our techno-angst, we instinctively take aim at its most visible emblem. Some of us do so harmlessly under our breath; others turn it into a showcase of juvenescence. With the spectacular success of Microsoft, with the understandable fixation on Gates's astounding personal fortune and with his conspicuous efforts to establish himself as the leading visionary of the personal computing revolution, Gates has been transformed into a potent cultural icon. He isn't just very rich and very famous. Like all dominant icons (Monroe, Reagan, Sinatra, etc.), he embodies an arresting social transformation. We look at him and we see our technological future, warts and all. As the upstart personal computing industry has blossomed into a computing-communications juggernaut, becoming—as of late 1997—the largest industry in the nation, we project onto Gates our hopes, fears, dark suspicions—but mostly our ignorance. We suddenly find ourselves fastened to an industry that we don't understand very well, but which rockets ahead regardless.

What then must be done? Any good tactician can tell you that the reasons for hating and fearing Microsoft must, however valid, be separated from the scheme to rein it in. The chorus of Microsoft-haters supplies a long list of reasons to hate the company: arrogance, hubris, duplicity, abuse of power. But, as with many past grassroots uprisings, animus toward Microsoft suffers from a lack of focus and misdirection that may ultimately render it vestigial. Unless the variegated band of detractors can come together to clearly articulate both a specific critique and a specific remedy, Microsoft-bashing will go the way of wisdom teeth and tonsils. It may live on forever, but to no real effect.

The rallying cry, suggests MIT researcher and software designer Philip Greenspun, should focus on the importance of innovation, and on Microsoft's apparent stifling of it over the last several years. Greenspun is the creator of the infamous Bill Gates Personal Wealth Clock, arguably the most elegant online jab at Gates. Here, Bill Gates's steroidal wealth—$41.0423 billion, at the moment this sentence was written—can be tracked minute by minute. The clock was designed, explains Greenspun, as a swipe at the man who has the gall "to make so much money writing software that ignores the users." But this is also Gates's secret weapon, Greenspun argues. Truly great software, he explains, perversely tends to be extremely vulnerable to competition, because it works so fluidly with other products and also because the programming code is made accessible to ensure compatibility. "If you're a bad engineer and you can't quite finish the specs and you think the specs aren't really needed, then you end up with a nasty pile of code with lots of bugs, a system where the guts depend on everything else"—where the software only works with programs created by the same sloppy engineers.

Thus, asserts Greenspun, Microsoft gets rich not despite the fact but *because* it produces inferior software. In a more just world, he says, "companies like Hewlett-Packard would be the winners because they make high-quality products. It's a shame that the Bill Gates we have is uninterested in technology. Consumers don't know what they're missing." According to this analysis, the real power of the information revolution has been to spur innovation about what technology can do for people. That inspiration has infected nearly everyone in the business like a virus, which is why everyone from sixteen-year-old webmaster James Baughn to MIT's Greenspun instinctively understands that, as spectacular as computing is right now, it is a mere fraction of what it *would* be if Microsoft didn't wield so much power.

This ethereal argument, repeated by Mitch Stone, Gary Reback, Andrew Shapiro, and most other serious critics, is the vaguest and yet by far the most compelling reason for anyone to hate and/or fear Microsoft. These critics want consumers, judges, and legislators to imagine an *It's a Wonderful Life* scenario in reverse: wondering what the world would be like without Bill Gates.

If critics instead stick to their current spate of hate, they may ultimately be doing Microsoft a great favor. For it is exactly this type of behavior, says Simson Garfinkel, that has helped Microsoft stay on top. "Lotus did great until they started focusing on Microsoft instead of focusing on their customers," says Garfinkel. "Netscape has made exactly the same mistake. Now Scott McNeally is making this competition with Microsoft very personal, swiping at every possible opportunity, rather than focusing on their customers. At the big Sun Java One conference a few months ago, McNeally's keynote was dedicated to why ActiveX, Microsoft's program, is a problem. That's really bad. You shouldn't make the keynote of your address bashing another company. And now Oracle's Larry Ellison is focusing on Microsoft instead of his own customers. Whenever a company does that, they lose."

Which means that, as long as Microsoft keeps its focus on itself, maintains that hungry feeling, and stays (more or less) within the bounds of the law, they're bound to succeed in business even as they inevitably inspire a continuing spiteful undercurrent. Of course, technology has a way of turning the tables rather suddenly. Regardless of Microsoft's foresight, toughness, breadth of investment, and research, Gates knows as well as anyone that his days as technology king could come to a fairly swift end. At that point, presuming that the end of his dominance would spur a plummet in the Microsoft stock price, he would become an underdog and, thus, a sympathetic figure. Letters would start pouring into editorial offices: "Stop picking on Microsoft!" Politicians would clamor to kiss his children. The Web would start crawling with "I ♥ Bill" sites. People would start arguing about who loved Bill the most.

A Few Moments with Mitchell Kapor

*Kapor is the founder of Lotus Development Corporation and co-
founder of the Electronic Frontier Foundation. He sent along a very
encouraging note when technorealism (which is discussed in detail in
part VII) was first introduced online and repeated his praise publicly at
a conference a few days later, dramatically disassociating himself from
the cyber-libertarian stance of his former EFF colleague John Perry
Barlow. He is now in the process of setting up a new nonprofit foundation that will focus on issues of technology and the public interest. I
have a tremendous admiration for the breadth of his social consciousness and his dedication to make technology serve humanity and not the
other way around. The following remarks of his are taken from a recent
telephone conversation.*

MITCHELL KAPOR: Too many people are seduced into the celebration of
high-tech and Silicon Valley as all which is excellent, and a view of
Microsoft as the engine of growth and success. There is an idolization
of technologies and the companies which produce the stuff—with the
covers of *Time* and *Newsweek* and *Fortune* and *Business Week* featuring
the latest, greatest thing. It really ought to be about value for regular
people who use this stuff to help with their lives. The technology falls
terribly short of where it could be today, where it should be. But there's
a lack of the ethic and commitment to that.

When you unhinge the things that hold the market in check, you
invite a situation that has many undesirable consequences. The problem is not in the Internet. The problem is, in my view, the lack of an
ethic, a social glue, that provides a basis for meaning in life other than
production and consumption. That's the central problem. Technologies amplify this, and in some ways enable it.

This is an eternal issue, one that manifests itself differently in each
era and epoch: *What is it that gives life meaning? What produces more
genuine happiness and less suffering?* Those are absolutely eternal
questions; they are the subject of every religion and underlie every
political philosophy. My view is that there is a hyperindividualism, a
set of social norms that is out of whack in its valorizing of individual

accomplishment. Why is Bill Gates such a huge hero? He is, as far as I can tell, completely unempathic with what regular folks who use computers go through.

What we don't have is a basis of solidarity that most people can feel genuinely good about. It ain't the labor movement. It's not an identification with the poor and the oppressed. Without a genuine, authentically felt base for solidarity, people are going to be unhappy, to feel disconnected, hollow. And technology sometimes winds up being used in the service of making things worse. But the problem is not amazon.com as much as it is that people are trying to buy happiness.

[*Technology Review*, March/April 1998]

To Mac or Not to Mac

One Apple Devotee's Excruciating Purchase Dilemma

Many years from now, I'll be hunched over in a creaky pine rocker on the porch of my retirement home. For hours at a time, I'll sit staring at the trees, lost in thought. Then a passing car will startle me out of my reverie and suddenly I'll begin to blurt out words like an old radio whose short-circuited wiring has accidentally righted itself. My utterances might seem incoherent at first, but whoever takes a moment to listen will quickly realize that they're not incomprehensible, merely ancient: "MacPaint . . . AppleShare . . . ImageWriter . . ."

I will tell anyone who pretends to listen, "I was a Mac person."

Maybe I'll get really lucky and catch the ear of a young history buff. She will recognize some of my strange utterings from her History of Technology class and understand right away that I come from the dawn of the Age of Personal Computing. With wide eyes and hushed voice, she'll want to know if I ever saw a Macintosh with my own eyes. I'll tell her truthfully and in all modesty, "I owned one."

The Mac will presumably be pure history by then. Every day seems to bring more bad news for Apple and its famously loyal customers: "Apple Loses $708M," "Apple to Slash Work Force by 30%," "Gateway 2000 Overtakes Apple in Education Market." One particularly dark moment came last fall, when Yale University officials declared that after 2000 the university network will not guarantee support for the Mac—until recently the most popular machine on campus. This public abandonment threatens to undercut Apple's strategy of falling back on a few niche markets, notably education; for longtime Apple users, it is a betrayal tantamount to telling an aging Nobel prize–winner that his services are no longer needed.

These, then, are tough times for any Mac person: to watch the steady demise of the company that invented this "insanely great" machine; to see frightened school principals and college deans abandon this elegant, intuitive platform; to see colleagues, friends, and even family members, good and loyal Mac people, throw in the towel, however valid their reasons—price, software selection, availability of peripherals. *Wired* magazine's cover story last year on the embattled company featured a collection of former Mac loyalists who have gone over to Windows for one reason or another. It was agonizing to read the list of high-profile defectors.

The question that has been disturbing me recently is *Should I join them?*

I realized a few months ago that I needed to buy a new computer. The last machine I bought was a Powerbook 180, purchased in 1993. It has a grayscale monitor, doesn't run a lot of Internet software, and, after four years of enthusiastic use, shows a fair amount of wear and tear. I try to avoid getting caught up in hardware and software upgrade mania—upgrading just for the thrill of it or in response to the pervasive cultural anxiety about falling behind. But sometimes there are good reasons to upgrade. Since I now perform a good portion of my research on the Web, it is time to step up to a quicker machine with color and more memory.

I phoned my brother Josh to tell him that maybe the time had come to switch to Windows: "Everyone else seems to be doing it."

"David," he gasped, "you're not serious!" This from someone who has been forced to use Windows at his place of business. Knowing that I have the freedom to stay with Mac, he couldn't believe I would even consider defecting.

It's not that I have become dissatisfied with the Macintosh. On the contrary: after thirteen years and nearly as many hardware upgrades or outright purchases, I retain my reverence for the machine that helps me think and write my best. The Macintosh was, after all, the first personal computer to capture the popular imagination. Before the Mac, nontechies didn't have much interest in personal computers for one simple reason—they weren't personal. They were *comput*ers—big ugly calculators that one could wrestle into performing calculations or type on without having to use Wite-Out™.

The Macintosh changed all that. Its famously intuitive graphical user interface, which put aesthetics on equal footing with function, turned the personal computer into a tool whose power derived not from its calculating capabilities (on that front, the Mac was no powerhouse) but from its ease of use. "The interface makes the teeming, invisible world of zeros and ones sensible to us," writes Steven Johnson in his terrific new book, *Interface Culture: How New Technology Transforms the Way We Create and Communicate.* "There are few creative acts in modern life more significant than this one, and few with such broad social consequences."

The cruel irony at work in the apparent disintegration of Apple is that as Mac has won the war of ideas, it has simultaneously lost the contest for financial preeminence to its imitators. "When Windows 3.0 swept the world, so did Apple's concept of beautiful software," writes Yale computer scientist David Gelernter in his book *Machine Beauty: Elegance and the Heart of Computing*. "Pushing beauty instead of old-fashioned DOS ugliness, Microsoft emerged as the uncontested leader of the desktop computing world." Currently, Windows has a 70 percent market share—to Mac's 7 percent—and is gaining.

In the face of that juggernaut, I told Josh, I felt it was important to keep an open mind. Mac users are frequently derided as zealots whose fiery devotion to the Mac defies all reason. I like to think of myself as fairly level-headed. I'd hate to look back on my life from that porch rocker and realize that I'd wasted fistfuls of money staying true to an increasingly inferior brand. I'd also be ashamed to discover that I had duped myself into ascribing more power to the Mac than it deserved. Maybe much of the magical feeling I have about the Mac is just wonder at the process of writing and the mysteries of creativity and intellectual growth—intangibles for which one is naturally tempted to find a totem.

For all these reasons, I resolved to consider Windows seriously. I called a few PC manufacturers and arranged to borrow some "Wintel" machines. I also called up Apple and told them that I was thinking about abandoning the Mac. Would they please cooperate by letting me borrow one of their hot new Powerbooks for a little while? They graciously agreed to assist me in my experiment.

For my preview of Windows 95, Toshiba sent me its Protégé 300CT and Fujitsu sent its Lifebook 655T. Both are four-pound notebooks that conveniently dock into CD-ROM/floppy drive units. I also spent some time with Gateway's P5-133 desktop. And what I found, much to my surprise, was this: Windows 95 is terrific.

Yes, I had my share of peripheral installation trouble and Internet connection trouble. I spent hours on the phone waiting for tech support and hours more actually talking to technicians as they helped me work out this or that kink. On the whole, getting going was somewhat more difficult than it's ever been with a Mac. But since neither platform is guaranteed to be headache-free, these differences don't mean much to me. If people want to live truly simple lives, they should avoid buying complex machinery.

Mac friends may toss virtual rotten eggs into my electronic mailbox for saying this, but I found Win95 to be wonderfully intuitive, even for someone who has spent many years getting used to another system. It didn't take much imagination to figure out that the Windows "Recycle Bin" works the same way as Mac's trash can; that instead of apple-P for "print," it's now control-P. Documents were easy to find, open, organize, duplicate, and send over the Internet.

In fact, I was startled to discover that a few Win95 features were clearly superior to their counterparts on the Mac. Using the all-purpose "Start" button in the lower left corner of the screen, for instance, I could effortlessly choose almost any function offered by the computer. And all windows can collapse to the bottom of the screen in an orderly fashion, making it easier to juggle lots of documents and programs at once. Even the much-touted Mac OS8 doesn't provide these seemingly obvious conveniences. (Mac's answer to window clutter is collapsible windows that suspend the title bars wherever they happened to be in the screen, a laughably useless gimmick.)

And then there's the guilty pleasure of being in Bill's corner. The Justice Department may not be too happy about Microsoft's market dominance, and as a consumer advocate, I'm not necessarily thrilled about it either. But as a plain old consumer, I *like* the fact that my operating system, word processor, Internet browser, email program, and scheduler are all designed by the same company to work in seamless synchrony. I *like* my software shopping to be a no-brainer, consisting simply of scouting for the Microsoft logo. I *like* my software company to be a financial titan, guaranteed to deliver timely upgrades on all my programs as long as I live.

More than anything else, discovering Win95's ease brings me an enormous personal sense of relief. As many of us have entered our second decade of Mac use, we've carried with us the deep fear that we are headed for oblivion, like romantic adventurers who find themselves driving off a cliff. Having sampled Windows 95 for myself, I now realize that Apple could crumble tomorrow and I would come out all right. David Gelernter is correct: the essence of Mac has swept the world. The war of ideas is over, and we're all winners.

Deciding whether to abandon the Mac is a two-part expedition.

Having answered question one—"Can I thrive with Win95?"—in the affirmative, I now faced question two: "Is there a compelling reason to leave Mac now?"

Answering this question, I have come to believe, is a matter of choosing the correct metaphor. Is buying a new Mac this year like buying a Porsche 911 or a Sony Betamax? Both are superior machines; neither boasts an impressive market share. Porsche parts may not be compatible with market leaders Toyota, Ford, and Honda, but they are nonetheless readily available (albeit pricey). Most important, the car rides beautifully on almost any road. Loyalty to the Porsche may seem eccentric, but the choice of driving system does not prevent one from getting where one wants to go or from enjoying the ride.

The Betamax, on the other hand, was a terrific machine that quickly lost its value for those who were unlucky enough to purchase one in the mid-1980s. A friend of mine in college clung proudly to his Betamax, touting its superior technology. But the vast majority of consumers chose the cheaper, if inferior, VHS machines, and Betamax "software"—videotapes—never developed into a viable market. My friend wound up playing the same few movies over and over again. Betamax proved that a superior technology can also be a useless technology if the market so dictates.

Some folks will say the Betamax analogy is the correct one here. It takes about ninety seconds in any software store to realize that there are vastly more titles available for Windows than for Mac. The Windows user has many more choices among peripherals such as printers and CD-ROM drives as well and tends to pay less to boot. Will Mac's 7 percent market share shrink inexorably to zero? If Mac is destined to slide into oblivion like the Betamax, I'd be a fool to buy one.

But to my mind, there are at least three good reasons why the Porsche analogy works and the Betamax analogy fails. First, Porsche may not be a top-selling car, but it sells well enough to keep lots of Porsche repair shops in business. Mac's 7 percent market share may not sound like much, but there are approximately twenty *million* Mac OS computers in operation right now. That's a substantial market by any measure, one that Microsoft and many other software and hardware vendors profit from handsomely. (Remember: Microsoft was producing and profiting from Mac software when there were fewer than a million Macs in circulation.) In fact, because of the enormous growth in the PC market, it's quite possible that even if the Mac market share slips to just a few percentage points over the next couple of years, the actual size of the Mac economy could keep on growing.

Even if Apple stopped selling Macs tomorrow, there would be a very healthy market out there for many years to come. Since Mac owners tend to use their machines longer than PC owners before upgrading, the Mac market is guaranteed to thrive at least through the end of the century.

Second, the Mac still has four wheels and chugs unleaded gasoline. That is, despite the apocalyptic visions conjured up by headline writers, it continues to provide the services that many of us are after (twenty million of us, apparently). Not only is the Mac still as user-friendly as complex machines come; it uses software similar or identical to the most popular applications available on Windows. As if to reinforce this point, Bill Gates publicly committed Microsoft last year to solid support for MS Office and Internet Explorer for the Mac for years to come. What has come to be unfairly regarded as an oddball specialty computer actually drives as well as anything else on the information superhighway.

Finally, it's a damn good car. I drive a Mac Powerbook for the same reason that car enthusiasts spend weekends behind the wheel of a 911: superior aesthetics, superior performance. We drive not just because we have to, but because we want to. We not only get to where we want to go; we also enjoy the ride.

That's not to say that there aren't other wonderful machines out there. But there's something very special about the Mac that people really seem to miss when they leave it behind (I've listened to their groans). Asking them to explain it is like asking a wine expert to explain the difference between a superb wine and a merely good one: It's a wordless experience. Those who come to Mac from Windows, like those who have never acquired a taste for fine wine, may never appreciate what they're missing. But to those attuned to fine distinctions, that indescribable difference is deeply significant.

The designers at Apple have always understood that the aesthetics of a computer are every bit as important as its technical performance and that a personal computer is not merely a tool but an extension of the user's mind and body. It assists and complements us in a range of subtle ways—it serves at once as notepad, Rolodex, and library; it adorns our desks; it is something we step into as we would a piece of clothing. Just as a superb meal always begins with pleasant lighting and the warm greeting of the maitre d', so it is that an exceptional computer is a pleasure to look at, listen to, touch—even before it's switched on.

The expensive and consequential task of choosing a computer involves a wide range of considerations, including compatibility, aesthetics, cost, comfort, and performance. A year or two before his celebrated return to Apple, Steve Jobs stirred up considerable turbulence when he revealed to the *New York Times* that, on a shopping excursion to buy his daughter a laptop for college, he was so disappointed in the Powerbooks that he bought her an IBM Thinkpad. Today, I think Jobs would buy his daughter a Powerbook, and not just because he is (as of the writing of this story) de facto chairman of Apple, but because the current line of Powerbooks is sensational. They are attractive, comfortable, quick, and mobile. Yesterday, I bought one myself—the new four-pound 2400/180c. I'm still getting used to the slightly cramped (but intelligently designed) keyboard but aside from that, it is everything you could ask for in a laptop: light enough to take everywhere and fast enough to keep me from rolling my eyes, with a vibrant active-matrix screen that can adjust to any angle even beyond 180 degrees, a long-lasting battery whose life can be enhanced in a variety of ways, and a case that is easy on the eye and to the touch. And in ways that perhaps only fellow Mac users will understand, it both expresses and evokes the fundamental human desire to create works that are not merely functional, but beautiful. With this machine, I expect to enjoy the ride for another several years.

Of course, few readers will have considerations identical to mine. As a freelance writer, I work alone in a freestanding home office. I don't use spreadsheets, I don't trade stocks, I don't play computer games. Mostly, I write articles and email and conduct research online. Although the Mac OS has made great strides in its effort to be compatible with Windows users, if I was thrust into a Windows-based office environment tomorrow, I'd probably be more inclined to use that platform. And I could do so, as I've discovered, with few regrets.

Still, Mac has that special "look-and-feel" that makes it worth the loyalty. In fact, my brother called the other day to say that in defiance of his workplace network, he is switching *back* to the Mac. He's figured out that all it will really take is a little extra disk-swapping from time to time.

Computers connect us to each other in important new ways, and no one would go out of their way these days to buy a computer that's truly incompatible with other computers. But for many of us, the far more important compatibility is that between the user and his or her machine. We spend an awful lot of time—most of our lives—trying to wrestle some creativity and intelligence out of these plastic boxes. We owe it to ourselves to try to make the enduring experience as fulfilling as it can possibly be.

[Personal conversation, December 7, 1998]

A Few Moments with Douglas Rushkoff

Rushkoff is a highly acclaimed author whose books include Coercion, Media Virus, Ecstasy Club, *and* Playing the Future. *In person, he's got a marvelous verbal energy that enables him to be highly articulate, detail-oriented, humanistic, and always entertaining. It's no surprise that Douglas is one of the most sought-after speakers on issues of technology and culture, and it was a great compliment when he leaned over to me in the middle of a conference last year and said that* Data Smog *had influenced him. Here's a one-sided excerpt from a recent conversation of ours.*

DOUGLAS RUSHKOFF: About six months before I read *Data Smog*, I switched from Mac to PC, and my life just got worse and worse as a result. That was about when my books started coming out in a whole bunch of different countries, and I started to get two hundred or three hundred emails a day. I started hating the computer. I felt controlled by it. And then your book comes out, and in reading your personal vision of it, I started to see that other intelligent people who were not anti-technology were somewhat saddened about how the promise of these technologies was being thwarted by various blindspots toward technology.

I look at information overload as a problem of filters—not technological filters but psychological/moral/ethical filters. Technology has given me the power to create the life I want for myself. And what I've got to do now is disengage from certain behavioral programs that are in place in my own brain, like "Earn as much money as you can," "Get as much work as the world will give you." Thanks to the Internet, there's more work available to me than I could possibly do. People get in touch with me all the time now and ask me to write things and do stuff. In the old days, people couldn't find me so easily. So basically what I have to do is to make some choices, and that's the thing that so many of us are uncomfortable doing—and so many of us didn't have to do before information overload. We could choose passively by what came to us and what didn't.

And because we've been inundated since childhood with the idea that the main method of self-expression is consumption, our information choices—which web pages we go to—say so much about who we are. This ethic forces us into an ongoing identity crisis. It's like the fourteen-year-old kid who doesn't know whether to get Nikes, Pumas, or Airwalks.

All these choices are, in the end, healthy. The bad thing is when people feel compelled, like they have to know things. The way to deal with this is to say: Hang on a minute. What is it you really *want*? Do you want to be online? Do you really want to know the price of tea in Bengal? Or do you want to spend time playing with your child?

vi.
generation next

Worries for Our Children

[*Wired*, December 1997]

School Bells and Whistles

Suddenly, education is more than a political hot button—it's one of the information industry's hottest new growth markets. Disney, for example, has been diversifying into "fun-filled learning" on the Web, "edutainment" CD-ROMs, and high-tech Club Disney multimedia centers whose business plan includes high-volume student traffic during school-day "field trips." Education Technology LLC, another major new edutainment outfit, is being backed by formidable profit seekers Larry Ellison and Michael Milken.

There is nothing inherently wrong with trying to make education fun, of course. It's almost impossible to learn in the absence of inspiration. The problem comes when we start pretending that good old-fashioned diversion can, with a few new charts and quizzes, easily be converted into something worth learning. We certainly want tomorrow's children to have more than a Mickey Mouse education.

"Use Technology to Raise Smarter, Happier Kids"

Behold the Toys of Tomorrow

"The killer app is the eyes," Erik Strommen tells me as he rotates his right hand to cover up two painted plastic eyes on the head of a plush, bright-purple dinosaur doll sitting placidly in front of us. The doll, about a foot long with a lime-green belly and six yellow toes, is a miniature replica of Barney, the popular children's television character; in place of the human being stationed within the polyester and foam of the life-size Barney, this rendition is packed with electronics and microprocessors courtesy of Microsoft. It's not alive, but it pretends to be. As soon as Barney's eyes are shielded from the light in the room by Strommen's hand, the doll reacts. "Whoa-oh-oh-oh!" Barney sings out in his familiar, punchy voice. "Where did you go?" When Strommen pulls his hand away, Barney blurts out, "Oh, there you are!"

"That's the killer app," Strommen repeats with a youthful grin. "The kids just can't get enough of that."

Here is one phrase I did *not* hear buzzing around the crowded showrooms and elevator wells at the 1998 Toy Fair, the frenzied annual New York City convergence of more than twenty thousand toy makers and toy sellers. At high-tech conventions such as COMDEX, "killer app" is one of those expressions that gets tossed out so often it tends to hang in the air like cigarette smoke. But not here, not yet. After all, this was only Microsoft's second year at Toy Fair.

Microsoft is so new to the toy industry, in fact, that it hasn't yet figured out a way to steal the show. I actually had a difficult time locating Microsoft's sales suite, finally chancing upon it at the end of a ninth-floor corridor, tucked away like an afterthought. Quietly, though, the software giant is off to an extraordinary start: the debut of ActiMates Barney, Microsoft's first toy, introduced in time for the 1997 Christmas buying season, was a smash success, with 350,000 units sold (at the premium price of $110) in its first six months. More importantly, the ActiMates toy line is shockingly innovative, clearly a harbinger of future playthings. Is Bill Gates on the verge of delivering the pulse and hubbub of the information revolution to my unsuspecting two-year-old? The prospect fills me and many other parents I've spoken to with a powerful mixture of hopeful curiosity and prickly anxiety.

"He looks like a plush doll," Strommen says of Microsoft's Barney, "but he's actually a cuddly little computer." The chief content developer for ActiMates, Strommen has brown hair with straight, cropped bangs, a broad smile, and a tendency to end declarative statements on an up note, as if he's asking a question. It's his way of politely making sure the listener is keeping up—of asking, "Are you still with me?" without actually saying the words. The rhetorical style suits his ambitious twenty-minute presentation, an amalgam of technical detail ("the technique is called horizontal overscan digital insertion"), multimedia Wow!, and daring educational pretension, all in service to the larger message: *This is not your father's teddy bear.* ActiMates Barney represents an entirely new class of toy, a "real category breaker," Strommen says. It's designed to be more of a nurturing companion than an amusing trifle.

From a hardware perspective, ActiMates Barney is clearly in uncharted toy territory: it has a PIC microprocessor/microcontroller with 192 kilobytes of RAM (more than my first PC), a two-megabit ROM chip, a transistor board, three motors, five sensors, and—most significantly—a two-way radio transceiver for wireless communication with television, videocassettes, and computers. Designed for kids aged two to five (the same demographic as the television show), Barney serves as a new sort of mediator for a toddler's interaction with the electronic world. A special radio signal, encoded into Barney TV broadcasts and built into a series of ActiMates CD-ROM software packages (software and transmitters sold separately), is detected and decoded by ActiMates Barney. As the show begins, the Barney doll sitting next to you or on your lap says, "I like watching TV with you," and then, "Here we go!" Soon it begins to respond coherently (if gratuitously) to the dialogue and images on the screen. During the course of any given program, the furry companion comments on the program content with steady bursts of affirmation ("This will be great fun!" "I like getting hugs!"); faux surprise ("Oh my!" "Look at that!");

and forced curiosity ("What is that?" "Let's look"). There are also partial sing-alongs, with the doll chiming in on choruses. Frequently, ActiMates Barney is simply giggling at or endorsing what the TV Barney is saying on screen:

> *TV Barney:* "Will you help protect our earth and keep it clean?"
>
> *ActiMates Barney:* "Yes!"

This provokes an instinctive creepy feeling in any adult who has never witnessed it before. After a while the agitation fades into annoyance, as the doll interrupts the television narrative with comments so consistently unnecessary that you'd probably worry if your own child were making them.

Apart from the TV and computer, ActiMates Barney functions as an "intelligent" stand-alone toy. Barney has a two-thousand-word vocabulary, sings seventeen songs, and plays twelve separate games. Squeeze his hand to play patty cake. Squeeze again to hear him meow like a cat, or play count-along. "I was bringing home early prototypes for my son to play with," Strommen says. "He loved it. We worked it into a bunch of our bedtime routines. For instance, if you don't do anything with Barney, he yawns, and then two minutes later he says, 'I'm sleepy—' and then 'Good night' as he powers down. So before bed, we used to take Barney in, sing a couple songs with him, and then just sit there and talk. Barney would yawn and say, 'I'm sleepy.' I'd say, 'Oh, it must be time to go to bed—Barney's sleepy.' Then Barney would go, 'Good night,' and my son would say, 'Good night, Barney.'"

Strommen's son is now four, and is beginning to outgrow Barney. Happily for him, his father has developed two new ActiMates dolls for the next level up. "We were Barney people, and now we're growing into Arthur and D.W. people," Strommen says of the new plush toys, who are also modeled on characters from a top-rated PBS show geared to ages four to eight. Arthur and D.W. are a brainy brother-and-sister pair—Arthur is the one with the nerdy glasses and awkward self-consciousness, D.W. the laughably precocious mop-head. The personalities differ, but the content of the two dolls is equivalent. With four-thousand-word vocabularies (twice that of Barney), they have more than a hundred phrases grouped into different categories—careers, tongue-twisters, holidays, and knock-knock jokes. "When we do testing," Strommen says, "usually at about the third or fourth knock-knock joke, the kid who's sitting next to me turns to me and says, 'I have one. Knock knock'—and we end up telling knock-knock jokes to each other. It's a real social activity. It gets kids thinking about what they know."

Strommen is a developmental psychologist by training (one of three psych Ph.D.'s on the ActiMates team), and an educational technologist in practice. Before coming to Microsoft in 1996 he spent seven years developing software for Children's Television Workshop. His seriousness of purpose comes shining through in his demonstration, in the dolls themselves, and in the accompanying software.

Strommen set out to develop a product that kids could interact with over a long period, and the hardware and software are indeed geared for a long-term relationship. Thanks to a calendar chip, Arthur and D.W. are able to track the time and date for the next ten years. They can be put to bed with your child, Strommen explains, and programmed to wake her in the morning with "Ding ding! Time to get up!" They can also "learn" and "remember" your child's birthday, for which they initiate a countdown sequence: "Five days to your birthday!" . . . "Four days to your birthday!" . . . and so on.

"He's like a little friend," I suggest to Strommen. He looks up at me and smiles. "Exactly," he says. "He knows you."

Toys that know you: here is an idea neither ahead of its time nor ten years too late, but which is right now perfectly, brilliantly ripe. Technologically, computers are just becoming small enough, powerful enough, and—with the recent popularization of wireless infrared links—communicative enough to fit anywhere and to record or transmit virtually anything. Economically, here are two separate industries, toys and computers, with impressive sales figures and large pools of creative talent, but also with flagging growth. Merge the two and suddenly you have a new market with a constantly replenishing source of fresh consumers and a pace of change speedy enough to attain that sublime condition of planned obsolescence. Venture capitalists spend their vacation days on the beaches of Cozumel fantasizing about synergies like this. Attaching microchips to squishy stuff is likely to make a lot of people very, very rich.

The computerization of toys also dovetails nicely with the ambitions of computer evangelists, those whose life's mission it is to deliver the power of computation into every aspect of every person's life. Nicholas Negroponte, the director of MIT's famously innovative Media Laboratory (the Vatican of techno-evangelism), noted last year in his *Wired* column that toys are the "fastest evolving vehicles on the infobahn," meaning that because of their astonishing turnover rate (each year, 75 percent of the toys on shelves are newly designed), they're the only class of objects that can truly keep up with the rapid pace of hardware and software innovation. That, combined with the tantalizing prospect of winning young, impressionable children over to the virtues of computers, has catapulted toy technology into high-priority status for the Media Lab. While researchers there have been exploring the issue for decades, they substantially upped the ante earlier this year with the formation of an industry-research consortium called Toys of Tomorrow. A dozen or so companies, including Mattel, Tomy, Intel, and Bandai (makers of the infamous Tamagotchi "virtual pets"), have signed up, committing to at least three years of the $250,000 annual sponsorship fee. In return for the funding (a modest R&D investment for any sizable company), sponsors get first crack at the new technology and ideas—a head start that seems bound ultimately to be worth many times that sum.

The promotional literature for Toys of Tomorrow is suffused with condescension toward objects (and their owners) still stuck in an analog world. "The digital revolution will transform the world of toys and play," the official TOT web brochure boasts. "Old toys will become smarter. New toys will become possible. All toys will become connected. There will be new ways of playing, designing, learning, storytelling. When a Cray becomes a Crayola, when a teddy bear sends a hug halfway around the world, when the beads on a child's necklace communicate with one another to make lights sparkle or music sound, we will be playing with the toys of tomorrow." Media Lab researchers are experimenting with a wide variety of wearable, musical, and communicative prototypes, and don't seem in any particular hurry to bring half-baked ideas to market. Most won't see the light of retail shelves for years.

One product, though, made its debut alongside the three Microsoft ActiMates dolls at last year's Toy Fair: the Lego MindStorms Robotics Invention System. The result of more than ten years of (pre-consortium) collaboration between the Media Lab and the Lego Company, Lego MindStorms is an advanced set of Lego bricks with motors, gears, and built-in sensors (light, touch, and infrared) that are coordinated by a small, mobile "programmable brick" computer brain. "You can build and program robotics invention systems that move and think on their own," the promotional literature promises.

MindStorms works much like any toy construction kit, with the additional component of some very basic computer programming. A child conceives an idea for a particular type of Lego-based robot (one that will deal playing cards to a certain number of players sitting around a table, for example, or that will "look" for a hockey goal and then shoot the puck), then assembles the bricks and gears into the desired structure, and programs the controlling brick by dragging and dropping icons using PC software. (The program is downloaded from PC to the Lego robot via infrared signal.) The project was originally inspired by Seymour Papert, a founding member of the Media Lab whose 1980 book, *Mindstorms: Children, Computers and Powerful Ideas*, is an impassioned treatise on how computers will enhance the intellectual development of children.

Mitchel Resnick, a forty-two-year-old associate professor at MIT and a protégé of Papert's, was the lead developer of the Lego Mind-Storms prototype and is one of the principals behind the Toys of Tomorrow project. When I visited Resnick at the Media Lab in Cambridge, his third-floor office was stuffed with so many large computer boxes that it was almost impossible to get inside. The cluster of hardware, Resnick explained, was earmarked for a major new exhibit at Boston's Computer Museum, called Virtual Fishtank. The exhibit, underwritten by a $600,000 grant from the National Science Foundation, allows visitors to create and interact with schools of computer-generated fish, which are programmed to react to the movement of people in front of the screen and to gobble up virtual food when it is "released" by onlookers. The fish also interact with one another in complex ways by following a few simple behavioral rules.

Virtual Fishtank is illustrative of Resnick's two overarching beliefs in the virtues of introducing computers to young children: (1) that computers can help kids understand dynamic systems in a way that traditional materials cannot; and (2) that the way to achieve these new levels of understanding is through creative design and construction.

"Traditional toys are good for young kids if they're trying to make sense of fundamental ideas like number, shape, scale, and color," Resnick says. "But there are other concepts having to do with the dynamics of the world—how things interact, how things change over time—that they aren't so good for. It's wonderful for kids to build all kinds of sculpture just with broken combs and forks and everyday items. It's harder to build *behaviors* with everyday materials. We emphasize using the computational materials where they give you leverage in dealing with things that involve some type of motion or interaction."

While his mentor Papert has made a career out of trying to convince people that computers will enormously expand the geometric thinking of human beings by provoking a mathematical curiosity at an early age, Resnick seems most interested in the proposition that cleverly designed machines can, paradoxically, help kids to better understand the complex dynamics of living things. "Let's say you're interested in how animals behave," Resnick says. "With modeling clay, or sand, or Lego bricks, you could build a model of a bunny rabbit. But the bunny rabbit is just going to sit there. You can make it look like a bunny rabbit, but you can't make it *behave* like a bunny rabbit. If you watch two rabbits playing with each other, you'll see there's a type of dance between them. How is it that they come to that dance? How is it that animals behave?"

Both the Lego robots and the Virtual Fishtank enable kids to confront these questions through creative design, Resnick argues. To demonstrate, he puts a couple of Legobots on the floor between us, a few inches apart from each other. At first they're completely immobile. "They look like they're not doing very much, but in fact they're sending out signals, and if they happen to see each other, they go into a little dance." As he says this, the two Legobots do "recognize" each other and start to jig back and forth. "Now, I don't think it would be very interesting to give these to kids as ready-made toys. That might be interesting for a few minutes, but it doesn't seem like a very deep play or learning experience. What's interesting is when kids can build up things like this. A child will say, 'I want the white one to tell the red one to start dancing.' He'll program that in, but then nothing will happen. So he'll say, 'Oh, the red one doesn't know *how* to dance, so I'll have to teach it.' When kids are going through that sort of activity, they're thinking about how to communicate. The hope here is that by building up their own communication models, kids start thinking about these ideas."

With his squinty smile, earnest intensity, and boyishly curly black hair, Resnick is both disarming and persuasive. He's so clearly trying to convince rather than sell that one is tempted to allow his sincerity to pass for proof. A similar feeling of indulgence follows a Media Lab visitor around on a tour, during which machines consistently seem to defy reality: coffee makers that recognize you by your magnetically encoded mug and customize your beverage accordingly; jean jackets with paper-thin music synthesizers sewn into the denim; wireless badges that communicate and keep track of social interactions; holograms that can be *felt* in three dimensions; bitmapped lightbulbs that cast designer shadows on a room. From the Herman Miller office chairs to the Jell-O-filled cloth instrument balls that produce different rhythms and intonations depending on how they are pulled and squeezed (one of many child instruments in development), the Media Lab is a Willy Wonka factory for technophiles, where the only limitations are in the creators' imaginations. Here computing not only transcends number-crunching, it also makes inanimate objects "think." Intoxicated by the MIT fumes, one thinks: How could this not be a boon to society?

In between Wow!s, though, I'm trying to remember that, like Wonka's sensational chocolate treats, these fantastic new devices for children can distract us from what ought to be our ultimate goal: improving the quality of our kids' lives, not just injecting more fun into them. Sherry Turkle, a prominent technosociologist also at MIT, argues that technology is fast propelling us into an entirely new paradigm of child development. "Today's children are growing up with 'psychological machines,'" she told the *New York Times* last June. "They have become accustomed to the idea that objects that are not alive might nonetheless have a psychology and even consciousness." If Turkle is correct, the critical question becomes: Do toys that think— or pretend to think—also spur our children to think?

Jean Piaget, the eminent Swiss psychologist who more or less invented modern developmental psychology earlier in the twentieth century, defined intelligence as the ability to cope with the changing world through the organization and reorganization of experience. The two critical and complementary ingredients of that adaptation, he proposed, are *assimilation*, fitting new information into an old conception of the world, and *accommodation*, devising a new conception of the world to fit new information that doesn't jibe with the old model. MIT's Seymour Papert, a student and a colleague of Piaget's in the late '50s and early '60s, developed his faith in the educational potential of computers from his own successful experience of assimilation as a child. His infatuation with the mechanics of a car, he says, evoked an intense level of mathematical curiosity at a very early age. "Gears, serving as models, carried many otherwise abstract ideas into my head," Papert writes in *Mindstorms*. "I saw multiplication tables as gears, and my first brush with equations in two variables (e.g., $3x + 4y = 10$) immediately evoked the differential." Since not everyone develops such a passion for car mechanics in particular, Papert reasons, children should have access to a machine that can adapt to their individual interests. "What the gears cannot do the computer might. The computer is the Proteus of machines. Its essence is its universality, its power to stimulate. Because it can take on a thousand forms and can serve a thousand functions, it can appeal to a thousand tastes."

Papert is correct to say that computers are pliable enough that they can be adapted to stimulate almost every child. But the transition from gears to computers invokes far more than the issue of customization. When an electronic toy is substituted for an immobile or mechanical one, the critical issue is not *whether* but *how* kids will be stimulated. A lifeless toy that doesn't speak or bleat or flash for attention may not reflexively draw every child's attention every time, but if it does, it will probably be for the right reasons—the child is curious, the child wants to explore. But what is the nature of the stimulation aroused by a set of squeezable balls that play exotic, electronic sounds? Or a playpen whose floor and walls are tripwired for different sounds? Is this stimulation or a form of neural captivation? Is the thinking toy sparking curiosity or mere amusement? "Up until recently," says Monty Stambler, a psychiatrist at Harvard Medical School and Boston's Children's Hospital and a toy developer himself, "toys have been animated by the imagination of their users. These toys turn that on its head. The electronic toy animates the user, instead of the other way around. That has to have an impact on creativity." The great danger with high-tech toys, then, is not that they won't excite children, but that the provocation will be of an unwanted—or unquantifiable—sort.

I voiced this concern to Resnick during my MIT visit. He is very sensitive to the idea that too much visceral stimulation can kill the creative impulse by subverting curiosity. One simply absorbs the flash of sound or light, is entertained and even hypnotized by it. There is an essential balance to be struck, Resnick agrees, wherein the tools are exciting enough to stimulate interest but are challenging enough to draw the user into a genuine intellectual pursuit. "We sometimes use a phrase around here—'hard fun'—that we've heard kids use when they're working with our products," he says. "We like to hear them use that term, because it's not meant to be easy. If it's too easy, if it's cotton candy, that's not what we want. At after-school workshops that we sponsor, a lot of the kids are working really hard, though no one is forcing them to. Kids who are seen as having attention problems in school will work for three straight hours on a project. Time and again we see that kids are willing to work hard at things that capture their imagination. So that's what we aim for, fun that is engaging but that has a type of depth to it."

From my own experience growing up with computers, I know that Resnick is speaking the truth. The notion of hard fun is real and meaningful, and is the basis for the most hopeful aspect of computer games, and of the Internet. The Net's ability to compel so many people to spend so much time forging personalized, electronic pathways of hyperlinks from subject to intriguing subject makes it the apotheosis of Papert's "Proteus of machines." Howard Gardner, the Harvard philosopher of education and the proponent of the theory of multiple intelligences, proposes that the key ingredient to a truly successful educational culture is the ability to appeal to and inspire the wide variety of abilities and combinations of intelligences that different people possess. This is the best argument I can think of for introducing computers and other thinking machines to children: to motivate kids by giving them the ability to design their own educational destinies.

Whether this new paradigm will present more opportunities than hazards, though, is another matter. Sherry Turkle has characterized the introduction of a machine consciousness into children's lives as a fundamentally social, fulfilling enterprise. As these psychological machines begin to pervade our culture, she says, kids "will be more likely to take the machines 'at interface value'—that is, to accept them as dialogue partners, even as companions of a sort." This echoes what Microsoft's Erik Strommen explained to me back at Toy Fair about the radical new role his toys will play in kids' lives. "These dolls are treated by children as if they are another person," he said. "They talk back to them, they laugh at their jokes. The dolls respond in a way that a good friend and a good learning partner would respond—they praise their successes, offer hints when you want them, that kind of thing." After our meeting, Strommen emailed me a paper elaborating on the nature of the companionship provided by his ActiMates dolls, which he equates with the bedrock developmental process of *scaffolding*. From his paper:

> Scaffolding is the process whereby an adult or more mature peer supports a child's acquisition of a new skill by providing assistance at key points during the execution of the skill itself, in a form of collaborative effort. An example of scaffolding might be helping a child learn to count by filling in numbers in the count sequence when the child is unable to remember them, or manually guiding the child's finger to each object being counted while counting along, to structure the task as it is executed. The metaphor of the scaffold is meant to capture the temporary and transitional nature of the learning intervention. Just as a scaffold is gradually removed from a new building as it is completed and can stand on its own, support of the child is gradually reduced as repeated effort leads to mastery of the new skill.
> . . .
> The goal of ActiMates Barney's design was to use the social mimicry of pretend play, combined with the differential responsiveness of interactive technologies, to provide scaffolded learning experiences for young children, both during toy play and in combination with other learning media.

I showed this to Harvard's Monty Stambler, who was horrified. Strommen's claim "does violence to the concept of what a scaffolding experience would be like," Stambler says. "All the sophistication of the adult is completely missing. He gives this example [elsewhere in the paper]: the child is supposed to pick the triangle and he gets the wrong one, and then Barney says to the child, 'A triangle has three sides.' He's calling that scaffolding—but that's not really what scaffolding is. That's *correcting*. Scaffolding is where you, the adult, start with what the child's perceptions are and work in a sort of Socratic method to help the child advance their understanding from where they are, individualized for them. What he's got here is formularized. It always says, 'A triangle has three sides.' There's no individualization, no calibration to where the child is at." (Other psychologists, including some cited in Strommen's paper, agree that his scaffolding claim is a wild stretch. It's "highly exaggerated," says Inge Bretherton, a psychologist at the University of Wisconsin. "I feel sad that he is citing my article in support of his claims.")

In Stambler's view, then, the so-called machine consciousness is bound to be nothing more than a thin facsimile of humanity. "It puts so much stress on learning fact and so little on feeling that it worries me," he says of ActiMates. "Do we want this Barney modeling our kids' involvement with television? I would find it objectionable to have a plush being unreservedly positive about a television program, because that's not how I am when I watch television. It's one thing when you're an adult and you know that it's just a feeling state that can be evoked and that it's not for real. It's another thing when you're a kid who's having this relationship with this talking plush. Emotional intelligence has certain components. One of them is a certain capacity to understand what someone else feels—the ability to link certain feeling states together, to know how to cope with a bad mood, and so on. These toys have no moods. Like Pinocchio, they're animated but they can't cry."

Of course, someday, Stambler allows, perhaps in time for our children's children, these toys may actually exhibit and read moods. Will they then place enough emphasis on real feeling to help kids navigate emotional terrain, or will the eerie proximity to humanity be all the more creepy and objectionable? Stambler's instinct is that there might be something beneficial there. I'm less sanguine.

What can we expect from the Toys R Us shelves of tomorrow? The fact that Stambler's harsh critique applies to some of the best-intentioned technologists in the toy business may ultimately be the most unnerving observation of all. Most of the toys of tomorrow, of course, will be as mindless and developmentally useless as most of the toys of today. A survey of Toy Fair's other high-tech entrants last year, though, raises the prospect that, because of the inherently captivating qualities of electronics, tomorrow's bad toys will be much, much worse. Exhibits A, B, and C: Toymax's "Mighty Mo" X-Treme Force S-10 Pick-Up, whose wireless key ring revs the engine and activates the car alarm;

Yes! Entertainment's handheld "Yak" sound-effects machines, which spit out an endless stream of distorted snarls, howls, and screams; and Play-Tech's "IQ Builders" series Professor Giggles, "the talking electronic toy that makes sentence structure (subject, object, verb) fun."

Erik Erikson, in his landmark 1950 book *Childhood and Society*, proposed that every culture socializes its children to uphold that culture's core values. What premier social value are we promoting with today's orgy of licensed character toys and electronic gizmos? In a word, Stambler says, *consumerism*. "Toys like these stunt creativity, make people dependent on animated objects to bring meaning into their lives, and make them constantly dependent on upgrades."

If we are already awash in consumerism, how bad could the future of toys really be? There is always a danger of gratuitous romanticism when we contemplate our future infrastructure—of reminiscing about the good old days that never were, instinctively fearing the richer, more complex world ahead simply because it is unknown. On the other hand, there is also the corresponding danger of pining for a world that can never be, cavalierly trading in the enormous achievements of the past and present for a look behind curtain number two. Our consumer culture may suffer from a confusion over life's priorities, but the good news is that, by and large, we already know as a society how to raise highly verbal, curious, and intelligent children. The ingredients for doing this turn out to be surprisingly low-tech: parents and their surrogates spending lots of individual time with kids, speaking to them very early on, playing music for them, providing a measure of security while allowing a measure of independence. There are many pitfalls, of course, and many children receive a far from ideal upbringing. But today's developmental deficits have little to do with the inability of children to master abstract mathematical thinking at a very early age.

As a first-time parent I have been struck repeatedly by the degree to which child-rearing is not, as I once thought, about raising the brainiest or most-athletic or most-musical children. Now that I actually have to make these choices, I find instead that I want to raise a confident, curious, patient, personable, humble, ambitious, generous, adaptable human being. Throughout the researching of this piece I found my parental intuition regularly confirming Monty Stambler's wariness of the high-tech, prepackaged entertainment units. Some of the more thoughtful toys of tomorrow will no doubt help to enlighten and provoke young minds into ways of thinking that are largely unavailable to my generation. But I'm confident that they will do nothing to advance the causes of child development that I now find myself passionately, paternally concerned with. And I'm afraid, even as an avid computer user, that if quasi-conscious electronic toys do begin to pervade our social space, something dear may be lost to us all. The great challenge of our age is to enjoy the benefits of technological advance without getting caught up in all of its tangles. As old toys become smarter, new toys become possible, and all toys become connected, we may discover that children adapt all too well to the souls of their new machines.

[*MSN*, December 1996]

Hall Pass to the Twenty-first Century

The Problem with Putting Schools Online

> Let's make education our highest priority so that every eight-year-old will be able to read, every twelve-year-old can log on to the Internet, every eighteen-year-old can go to college. We can build that bridge to the twenty-first century.
>
> —Bill Clinton

Breathe easy about our education crisis. The cavalry has arrived. In case you hadn't heard, it's the Internet that is going to save our schools.

The information superhighway is going to deliver unto us "a new generation of geniuses," promises Microsoft chairman Bill Gates. Newt Gingrich is confident that computers and the Net will serve as salvation for the underprivileged. And Messrs. Clinton and Gore have made wiring the schools the cornerstone of their education policy. If we follow their prescription, they say, we will experience a "revolution in education."

Seriously, though: is the Net really our penicillin which will forevermore ward off the ravages of ignorance? Should access to the Web be considered as important a priority as teaching someone to read?

No. We're getting caught up in the excitement of these spellbinding tools. Flushed with bandwidth, we have confused "information" with "knowledge." For the sake of our children, if no one else, it is a mistake that we must correct.

Apple Computer co-founder Steve Jobs has been down this road before. "I used to think that technology could help education," said Jobs in 1996. "I've probably spearheaded giving away more computer equipment to schools than anybody else on the planet. But I've had to come to the inevitable conclusion that the problem is not one that technology can hope to solve. . . . You're not going to solve the problems by putting all knowledge onto CD-ROMs. . . . Lincoln did not have a web site at the log cabin where his parents home-schooled him, and he turned out pretty interesting. Historical precedent shows that we can turn out amazing human beings without technology. Precedent also shows that we can turn out very uninteresting human beings with technology."

Jobs has it exactly right. Though computers can be useful tools in education, if used carefully and thoughtfully, they are by no means an educational necessity. The process of creating intelligence is not merely a question of access to information. Would that learning were as easy as diving into a swimming pool of information or sitting down at a great banquet table for an info-feast. Rather, education, which comes from the Latin *educo, educare,* meaning to raise and nurture, is more a matter of imparting values and critical faculties than inputting raw data. Education is about enlightenment, not just access.

There is, therefore, a much more serious danger than letting our schools languish in outdated technologies: it is pretending that cutting-edge technologies will serve as a substitute for a sound physical infrastructure and top-flight teaching. Computers by themselves cannot teach us to think critically, to be skeptical, rational, open-minded, and curious. These are human values that require human instruction.

No responsible teacher in the 1970s would ever have dropped off a class at the Library of Congress and said simply, "Go learn." The dynamic is no different with our new electronic library.

Nonetheless, we will continue to hear much about the educational glories of the Internet, from politicians who recognize it as a seductive and relatively cheap solution, and from industry leaders who stand to gain much from the hype. One of the first lessons we can teach our kids, in fact, is to think critically about their well-spoken patrons from Washington, D.C., and Silicon Valley. How can we best build that bridge to the next century? By teaching every eight-year-old to read, every twelve-year-old to be skeptical about what he or she reads, and every eighteen-year-old to distinguish corporate hype from reality.

[*MSN*, December 1996]

Stupid Kid-Tricks

The Actual State of "Educational" Material Online

I'm ten years old, searching for organic knowledge on the Web. Free from the restraints of conventional schooling, I can chart my own path, learn at my own pace, weave my own web of intellect. I am ChildWeb-surfer; watch me splash.

This freedom of movement is thrilling. The problem is that it doesn't come with any quality assurance. And what do I know from reliability or credibility? I'm only ten.

But who cares. I won't be aware of this concern until well into the next century. For now, I am on an electric educational safari. My first hunt is for information about the environment. Follow my path:

I go from the Yahoo page –> "Yahooligans!" –> School Bell –> Homework Answers –> Environment –> Plastic Bag Information Clearing House.

This page reads: "Welcome to the Plastic Bag Information Clear-inghouse, your resource for reliable information about plastic bags and the environment. . . . do you know whether paper or plastic bags create more waste?"

I don't know—but I am excited to learn. I click to test my "environ-mental IQ," and wind up answering fun questions to an online puzzle. Whenever I get the questions correct, the puzzle pieces turn over to reveal a hidden image.

Here's what I learn from every puzzle question: plastic is much more environmentally friendly than paper.

Here's what I will realize many years from now, when I am a more skeptical thinker: this quote-unquote "For Kids Only!" educational web site has been rigged by its sponsor, a consortium of plastic companies. Then I will combine that fact with this one: according to Beth Edwards, Yahoo's director of brand management, most of the traffic on "Yahooligans!" comes from schools.

"Classroom Connect" is another popular educational site. Let's go there.

One of the first things I notice is that, unlike my boring textbooks in school, "Classroom Connect" pages feature interactive advertising. Fun for me, but I'm not too sure my parents would be thrilled to hear about that.

My teacher instructed me to look only at the highest-rated educational sites, so I am restricting myself to "Classroom Connect's" "A+" list. Here's a site called "The Froggy Page." That looks fun—ooh, cool: "The Froggy Page" features a link to "The Pad," the homepage of the Budweiser frogs. At this site, I can learn how to prompt the three frogs—Bud, Weis, and Er—to make their trademark sounds. Maybe this is an education lesson on how to direct my own television commercial. A+ stuff.

The art division of Classroom Connect takes me to a site featuring Calvin and Hobbes, and another telling me everything I could possibly want to know about Mr. Potato Head. It also features something called "greykidwatch" which, after some poking around, I discovered was sponsored by Grey Advertising. They wanted me to fill out a questionnaire in their Cool World about things I liked and didn't like, and they offered a tour of their Haunted Candy Factory.

I said no thanks. I've been spooked enough already for one afternoon.

[*Harper's*, December 1997]

Biocapitalism

What Price the Genetic Revolution?

About a year ago, my wife phoned to say that something might be wrong with our unborn child. A blood test suggested the possibility of Down syndrome, and the doctor was recommending amniocentesis and genetic counseling. As it happened, I was almost finished writing a book about the paradoxical nature of information technology—the strange realization that more, faster, even better information can sometimes do more harm than good. When my wife's obstetrician reported the alarming news, it seemed as though the God of Technology was already looking to settle the score. The doctor, after all, was merely reading from a computer printout. Test results poured over us in a gush of formulas and statistics. My wife's blood contained such-and-such a ratio of three fetal hormones, which translated statistically into a such-and-such increased chance of our child having an extra chromosome, a forty-seventh, which can cause severely limited intellectual capacity, deformed organs and limbs, and heart dysfunction. The amniocentesis would settle the matter for certain, allowing a lab technician to count the fetus's actual chromosomes. But there was a dark statistical specter here, too, a chance that the procedure itself would lead to a spontaneous miscarriage whether the fetus was genetically abnormal or not. Testing a healthy fetus to death: many times in the days ahead, I wondered if I could come to terms with that ultra-contemporary brand of senselessness. The computer thought it a risk worth taking: the chance of miscarriage was slightly lower than the chance of discovering Down syndrome. My wife and I put our faith in the computer.

Few of these details will seem familiar to parents of children born before this decade; nor will any parents of children born after, say, 2010 face our specific predicament. The discoveries in the field have been generating one astonishing headline after another about genes related to Alzheimer's, breast cancer, epilepsy, osteoporosis, obesity, and even neurosis; the fetal-genetics revolution is now so accelerated that remarkable technologies become obsolete almost as quickly as they are invented. Although the "triple marker" blood test was invented in the late 1980s, it probably will be a historical footnote a decade or so from now. So will amniocentesis. Both will be replaced by a genetic sampling of fetal cells extracted from the mother's blood, a test that will be risk-free for both mother and fetus. That's hundreds of healthy fetuses every year who will not be lost just for the sake of a genetic snapshot. We will know much more for much less.

But the odd question arises: will we know too much? Fetal and embryonic genetic karyotypes may ultimately be as legible as a topographical map: Your son will be born healthy; he will be allergic to cashews; he will reach five foot ten and a half inches; math will not come easily to him; in his later years, he will be at high risk for the same type of arteriosclerosis that afflicted his great-grandfather. Here are secrets from the heretofore indecipherable text "The Book of Man," the wishful term used by researchers to refer to the complete translation of human genetic information that they one day hope to acquire. Such a discovery is what C. S. Lewis foresaw when he warned, in a prescient 1944 essay "The Abolition of Man," "The final stage is come when Man by eugenics, by prenatal conditioning . . . has obtained full control over himself."

I'm jumping ahead, far beyond present facts and into the future. "The Book of Man" will not be finished for some time, if ever. But with the U.S. government's staunch support of the Human Genome Project, the $3 billion mega-research sprint to map out and decode all of the estimated 100,000 human genes by the year 2005, genetic knowledge has suddenly become a national priority. It is this generation's race to the moon, but we're not quite sure what we'll do when we get there; what the dark side looks like most of us don't particularly want to imagine.

We're pursuing the human genome for good reasons, of course. With our new syllabus of genetic knowledge, we will become healthier and live longer. But even with the few facts that we now have, there is already cause to worry about the unintended consequences of acquiring such knowledge. If genes are the biological machine code—the software—containing the instructions for each person's development and decay, unlocking that code portends the ability to fix the bugs and even to add new features. When people worry aloud that we may soon be "playing God," it's because no living creature has ever before been able to upgrade its own operating system.

Lewis suggests that such absolute biotechnological power is corruptive, that it robs humanity of its instinctive duty to posterity. "It is not that they are bad men," he writes of future genetic "Conditioners." "They are not men at all. Stepping outside the Tao"—that is, outside the moral order as dictated by Nature—"they have stepped into the void." Although not yet close to a moral void, we do, even at this primitive stage of biotechnology, effortlessly step outside the Tao. Consider, for example, that when my wife and I went in for amniocentesis, we did so with the tacit understanding that we would abort our child if we discovered that he or she was carrying the extra chromosome; otherwise, there would have been no point in risking miscarriage. The fact that we did not abort our child, that she was born healthy, with forty-six chromosomes and four chambers in her heart and two lungs and two long legs, is morally beside the point. We had made our if-then choice to terminate. I suppose I'm glad I had the legal freedom to make that choice; I know, though, that I'm still haunted by the odd moral burden it imposed on me: Here is a preview of your daughter. If she's defective, will you keep her?

We all want a world without Down syndrome and Alzheimer's disease and Huntington's chorea. But when the vaccine against these disorders takes the form of genetic knowledge and when that knowledge comes with a sneak preview of the full catalog of weaknesses in each of us, solutions start to look like potential problems. With the early peek comes a transfer of control from natural law to human law. Can the U.S. Congress (which seems intent on shrinking, not expanding, its dominion) manage this new, enlarged sphere of influence? Can the churches or the media or the schools? To mention just one obvious policy implication of this biotechnological leap beyond the Tao: the abortion debate, historically an issue in two dimensions (whether or not individuals should have the right to terminate a pregnancy), suddenly takes on a discomfiting third dimension. Should prospective parents who want a child be allowed to refuse a particular type of child?

From that perspective, I wonder if today's crude triple marker/amnio combination isn't just an early indication of the burdens likely to be placed on future generations of parents: the burden of knowing, the burden of choosing. I imagine my daughter, pregnant with her first child. The phone rings. The doctor has reviewed the karyotype and the computer analysis. He is sorry to report that her fetus is carrying a genetic marker for severe manic-depressive illness, similar in character to that of my great-uncle, who lived a turbulent and difficult life. Will she continue the pregnancy?

Or perhaps she is not yet pregnant. In keeping with the social mores of her day, she and her partner have fertilized a number of eggs in vitro, intending to implant the one with the best apparent chance for a successful gestation. The doctor calls with the karyotype results. It seems that embryos number 1 and 6 reveal a strong manic-depressive tendency. Will my daughter exclude them from possible implantation? The choice seems obvious, until the doctor tells her that embryos 1 and 6 are also quick-witted, whereas 2 and 3 are likely to be intellectually sluggish. The fourth and fifth embryos, by the way, are marked for ordinary intelligence, early-onset hearing impairment, and a high potential for aggressive pancreatic cancer. Which, if any, should be implanted?

Now add a plausible economic variable: suppose that my daughter gets a registered letter the next day from her health maintenance organization, which also has seen the karyotype and the analysis (both of which they happily paid for). The HMO cannot presume to tell her which embryo to implant, but she should know that if she chooses to implant embryo number 1 or 6, the costs of her child's manic depression will not be reimbursed, ever. Now that the genetic marker is on the record, it is officially a "pre-existing condition" — in fact, the term has never been more appropriate.

Such are some of the specific scenarios now being bandied about by bioethicists, who, because of the Human Genome Project, are flush with thinking-cap money. Five percent of the project's funds (roughly $100 million over fifteen years) is being dedicated to social and ethical exploration, an allotment that prompted Arthur Caplan, director of the University of Pennsylvania's Center for Bioethics, to celebrate the HGP as the "full-employment act for bioethicists." The Department of Energy, the National Institutes of Health, and the international Human Genome Organisation all have committees to study the social and ethical implications of genetic research. Popping up frequently are essays and conferences with titles like "Human Gene Therapy:

Why Draw a Line?" "Regulating Reproduction," and "Down the Slippery Slope." While genetic researchers plod along in their methodical dissection of chromosomes, bioethicists are leaping decades ahead, out of necessity. They're trying to foresee what kind of society we're going to be living in when and if the researchers are successful. In Sheraton and Marriott conference halls, they pose the toughest questions they can think of. If a single skin cell can reveal the emotional and physical characteristics of an individual, how are we going to keep such information private? At what level of risk should a patient be informed of the potential future onset of a disease? Will employers be free to hire and fire based on information obtained from their prospective employees' karyotypes? Should a criminal defendant be allowed to use genetic predisposition toward extreme aggressiveness as a legitimate defense, or at least as a mitigating factor in sentencing?[1] Should privately administered genetic tests be regulated for accuracy by the government? (Currently they are not.) Should private companies be able to patent the gene sequences they discover? Should children of sperm donors have the right to know the identity and genetic history of their biological fathers? The only limitation on the number of important questions seems to be the imagination of the inquirer.

Most fundamental of all, though, are questions regarding the propriety of futuristic gene-based medical techniques. Suppose for a moment that the power to select on the basis of, and possibly even alter, our genetic code does, as many expect, turn out to be extensive. What sort of boundaries should we set for ourselves? Should infertile couples be allowed to resort to a clone embryo rather than adopt a biological stranger? Should any couple have the right to choose the blond-haired embryo over the brown-haired embryo? Homosexuality

---

1. This question is not hypothetical. In February 1994, Stephen Mobley was convicted of murder and sentenced to death. In their appeal, Mobley's lawyers argued that he had inherited a strong predisposition toward aggression. The appeal was rejected. But Deborah Denno, professor of law at Fordham, believes that genetic evidence will be admitted into U.S. courts within a few years. "Given that so many people who commit homicides also have histories of families with relatives who are also incarcerated," she said in the *London Independent*, "I think it's just a matter of time before somebody tries it again."

over heterosexuality?[2] Should we try to "fix" albinism in the womb or the test tube? Congenital deafness? Baldness? Crooked teeth? What about aortas that if left alone will likely give out after fifty-five years? Should doctors instead pursue a genetic procedure that would give the ill-fated embryo a heart primed for ninety-nine years?

To address these questions, bioethicists need to determine what competing interests are at stake. If a father wants a blue-eyed, stout-hearted son and is able to pay for the privilege, which will cause no harm to anyone else, what's the problem? Consider the prospect of a pop-genetics culture in which millions choose the same desirable genes. Thousands of years down the line, the diversity in the human gene pool could be diminished, which any potato farmer can tell you is no way to manage a species. While public policy generally arbitrates between individual rights and social responsibilities, genetics raises a new paradigm, a struggle between contemporary humanity and our distant descendants.

The considerable support for legislation that would suppress some of these technologies draws its strength from a sense of moral indignation as well as from the fear of an alien future. In a *New Republic* essay, "The Wisdom of Repugnance," University of Chicago philosopher Leon Kass argues for a permanent ban on human cloning, a ban grounded not in hysteria but in moral principle. "We are repelled by the prospect of cloning human beings not because of the strangeness or novelty of the undertaking," he writes, "but because we intuit and feel, immediately and without argument, the violation of things that we rightfully hold dear."

On the other end of the spectrum, some scientists argue against any boundaries, proposing that whatever we can do to better ourselves is not only ethically appropriate but also imperative. "The potential medical benefits of genetic engineering are too great for us to let

---

2. Dean Hamer, chief of the National Cancer Institute's gene structure section, claims to have discovered genetic markers for behaviors such as sexual preference, thrill seeking, and neuroticism. "Psychiatrists making diagnoses and prescribing drugs in the future will look at patients' DNA, just the way they now ask about family history," Hamer has said. Other geneticists cast doubt on these studies after failing to confirm the correlation between genetic markers and behaviors in follow-up studies.

nebulous fears of the future drive policy," argues Gregory Stock, director of the Center for the Study of Evolution and the Origin of Life at UCLA. Stock and others contend that we know better than Nature what we want out of life, and we owe it to ourselves and future generations to seek genetic improvement as a component of social progress. In his article "Genetic Modifications," for example, Anders Sandberg, a young Swedish scientist and self-described "Transhumanist," not only recommends the removal of genetic "defects" and such less harmful "undesirable traits" as drug abuse, aggression, and wisdom teeth but proposes a wide selection of enhancements to benefit the entire race. Systemic improvements would involve reprogramming cells to be more resistant to aging, toxins, and fat. "Cosmetic modifications" would be the plastic surgery for the next millennium—alteration of hair color or texture, eye color, skin color, muscular build, and so on. Sandberg even fancies deluxe new features such as built-in molecular support for frozen cryonic suspension. We can chuckle now at the improbability of these ideas, but when we do we might also try to imagine how people might have reacted 150 years ago (before electricity, before the telegraph) to someone suggesting that people in the late twentieth century would routinely converse with people on other continents using portable devices the same size and weight as an empty coin purse. "It basically means that there are no limits," Princeton biologist Lee Silver remarked after the announcement of Dolly, the cloned sheep. "It means all of science fiction is true. They said it could never be done and now here it is, done before the year 2000."

The attitude within the ranks of the Human Genome Project community is, not surprisingly, quite a bit more conservative than Sandberg's. Nowhere in the project summaries will an affiliated researcher be found yearning publicly for a world filled with fat-proof, freezable people (although no one seems to have misgivings about any conceivable genetic engineering of pigs, cows, or other non-humans). More modestly, the stated hopes for the application of gene mapping include a greater understanding of DNA and all biological organisms; new techniques for battling genetic diseases; a new prevention-oriented type of medicine, and a windfall for agribusiness and other biotech industries.

The fact that researchers are careful to limit their publicly stated goals reflects not so much a deeply ingrained social ethic, says Arthur Caplan, as a canny political awareness. "If uncertainty about what to do with new knowledge in the realm of genetics is a cause for concern in some quarters," he writes in the book *Gene Mapping*, "then those who want to proceed quickly with mapping the genome might find it prudent to simply deny that any application of new knowledge in genetics is imminent or to promise to forbear from any controversial applications of this knowledge. . . . [This] is the simplest strategy if one's aim is not applying new knowledge but merely to be allowed to proceed to acquire it." Caplan thus exposes a built-in tension between researchers and ethicists. Ethicists are paid to arouse concern, but researchers lose funding if too many people get too worried.

Spotlighting the personal motivations of their researcher counterparts might seem a little beyond the purview of bioethicists, but in fact bioethicists are obliged, as part of the exploration of propriety, to not only hope for the ideal social circumstances of genetic engineering but also to consider the more probable landscape for it, an approach we might call "realethik." To simply declare certain procedures immoral and call for an immediate and permanent ban is to ignore brazenly the history of technology, one lesson of which might fairly be summarized as "If it can be done, it will be done." E.g., the atomic bomb. The genie found its way out of that bottle in short order, almost instantaneously revolutionizing the way we think about conflict. Realethik dictates that other genies will escape from their bottles no matter what we do to stop them. Glenn McGee, a Caplan protege at the University of Pennsylvania and the architect of what he calls a "pragmatic approach" to genetics, argues that while we may be able to revolutionize our technology, there is no escape from human nature. We're wasting our time, says McGee, huffing and puffing about an international ban on human cloning. "Get over it. It's not going to happen. We are fundamentally in an unpoliceable realm." Human cloning will occur, probably in Chelsea Clinton's lifetime. And considering the current trajectory of genetic research, so will a host of other exotic and frightening developments.

If one accepts McGee's worldview, genethical considerations shift abruptly from policies of stark authorization/prohibition to a web of regulation and incentive, from ultimatums to real diplomacy, from grandstanding to nuance and compromise. Instead of regarding advanced genetic engineering as taboo, as a eugenic catastrophe waiting to happen, one plunges straight into the facts, and works to maximize the general social welfare and to minimize harm. From the pragmatic perspective, the warning about "playing God" is a distracting irrelevance, since we're already playing God in so many ways. In Escondido, California, for example, the Repository for Germinal Choice, a.k.a. the "Nobel sperm bank," collects and distributes sperm from an exclusive group of extraordinary men—top athletes, scientists, executives, and so on. A number of clinics in the United States now enable prospective parents to sex-select their children in advance of fertilization, sorting "male" (Y chromosome) sperm from "female" (X chromosome) sperm according to their volume and electrical charge, with an estimated success rate of 90 percent.

What about the horrifying prospect that parents might react irresponsibly to the genetic sneak preview of their fetus or embryo? That genie has escaped already, too. In what has become a powerful cautionary tale in bioethicist circles, an American couple was advised recently that their fetus had a rare extra chromosome that would not cause a debilitating disease like Down syndrome but that potentially, possibly, was linked to tall stature, severe acne, and aggressive, even criminally aggressive, behavior. The couple responded to this information by aborting their child. Their decision was ice water in the face of bioethicists, who concluded that the couple should not have been informed of the unusual, vague condition. The hard truth, says McGee, is that "when given the opportunity, people can do things that are inappropriate and unwise."

This inescapable element of human nature is why industrialized societies that respect the basic freedoms of their citizens nonetheless impose so many niggling restrictions on them—speed limits, gun control, waste-disposal regulations, food-and-drug preparation guidelines, and so on. As technologies advance further, conferring even more power and choice on the individual—the abilities to travel at astonishing rates of speed, to access and even manipulate vital pieces of information, to blow up huge structures with little expertise—societies will have no option but to guard against new types of abuse. Realethik is, therefore, inevitably a prescription for aggressive and complex government oversight of society and its powerful new tools.

Scratch the surface of both the information and biotech revolutions, in fact, and what one discovers underneath is a "control revolution," suggests political theorist Andrew Shapiro, a massive transfer of power from bureaucracies to individuals and corporations. In an unregulated control revolution, free markets and consumer choice become even more dominant forces in society than they already are, and in virtually every arena social regulation gives way to economic incentive. Unrestrained consumerism augments the ubiquitousness of pop culture and the free-for-all competition for scarce resources. Ultimately, even such social intangibles as privacy become commodified.

The unpleasant extremes of this climate are not very difficult to imagine: an overclass buying itself genetic immunity from industrial waste, leaving the working class gasping in its wake; conglomerates encoding corporate signatures onto genetic products, rendering competing products ineffective and enforcing the ultimate brand loyalty; parents resorting to all available legal means to ensure their kids can compete effectively, including attempts to, in the parlance of the Repository for Germinal Choice, "get the best possible start in life." In the absence of legal restrictions, one envisions the development of a free-market eugenic meritocracy—or, to coin a term, biocapitalism. If left up to the marketplace, designer genes could even allow the wealthy to pass on not only vast fortunes but also superior bioengineered lineages, thereby exacerbating class divisions.

With that much freedom and independence, the paradoxical question one must finally ask is, Can freedom and independence, as we know them, survive? The genetic revolution may well deliver the apex of "life, liberty, and the pursuit of happiness," but it seems destined to conflict with another bedrock American principle. Two centuries after it was first proclaimed, we still abide by the conceit—the "self-evident" truth—that "all men are created equal." We know, of course (as did our founding fathers), that this is not literally true: people are born with more, less, and different varieties of strength, beauty, and intelligence. Although we frequently celebrate these differences culturally, from a political and legal standpoint we choose to overlook them. For the purposes of sustaining a peaceful, just, and functional society, we are all considered equal.

An unregulated, unrestricted genetic revolution, by highlighting our physical differences and by allowing us to incorporate them in our structures of enterprise, might well spell the end of this egalitarian harmony. In this pre-genetics era, we are all still external competitors, vying for good jobs, attractive mates, comfortable homes. After the revolution has begun in earnest, much of the competition will likely take place under the skin. We will compete for better code. Such a eugenic culture, even one grounded in a democracy, will inevitably lead to the intensified recognition and exaggeration of certain differences. In a newly human-driven evolution, the differences could become so great that humans will be literally transformed into more than one species. But even if this doesn't happen, our thin metaphysical membrane of human solidarity might easily rupture under the strain. "The mass of mankind has not been born with saddles on their backs," Thomas Jefferson wrote two centuries ago, "nor a favored few booted and spurred, ready to ride them . . ." Who today can consider the momentum of genetic research and be confident that in another two centuries Jefferson's words will still hold true?

[*Feed*, July 1998]

Be Afraid

(Written in reaction to an announcement that more than fifty mice had been successfully cloned at the University of Hawaii.)

Be afraid. Last week's astonishing news that two scientists in Hawaii have cloned more than fifty mice, that they have essentially perfected the process introduced by Ian Wilmut last year (it got to the point where they were creating a cloned mouse embryo each day), is confirmation that the morality of family planning is about to become a lot more tangled. Wilmut's Dolly was the warning shot. Ryuzo Yanagimachi's batch of coffee-colored mice is the signal that the world now has an honest to goodness recipe for human cloning. Any takers?

Both the writing on the wall and the writing in the *New York Times* indicate that human cloning is imminent—if not in time for the millennium (*Happy Birthday, Futureboy!*), then very shortly thereafter. "Absolutely, we're going to have cloning of humans," says Princeton's Lee Silver, a leading geneticist and one of the most overtly sanguine. In fact, it seems that the only thing to have evolved faster and further than the science of cloning since February 22, 1997, is our social disposition toward human cloning. "We have no interest in cloning humans," one venture capitalist setting up a cloning company told the *Times* last week. "Besides being the politically correct answer, we can't see any business in it." In the span of eighteen months, then, cloning humans has gone from unthinkable to merely unprofitable.

And how far away can economic viability be? A recent *Nightline* featured two geneticists arguing that cloning could be a reasonable option for infertile couples. Sitting in the contrary seat was a shrill Christian theologian who kept repeating rather unhelpfully that the very notion was preposterous. The audience was made to understand that, as otherworldly as the idea of the two-parent, two-clone family may seem today ("My, Andrew, how you have grown into a spitting image of your father"), reasonable people will eventually get used to it. Before not too long, *au courant* magazine writers will offer parenthetical dismissals of stodgy genetic refuseniks who are stuck in oldthink.

Of course, human cloning isn't necessarily bad just because it's such a mindblower. There may indeed be some appropriate uses for it. But how are we going to determine what they are? What is clear even now is that the moral convolutions we will soon be facing—not just regarding cloning but also with respect to a wide variety of tests and alterations of genes in adults, fetuses, and gametes—are beyond the capacity of our current social discourse. Our specialized tools are increasingly more sophisticated than our discussion about their use. A formal national dialogue, along the lines of Clinton's race dialogue but with candor, seems urgent. Secondary-school curriculum must be significantly beefed up as well. Finally, we might also seriously consider Danish-style consensus conferences, where geneticists, ethicists, policy-makers, and ordinary citizens would be thrown together to formally study and discuss the issues and then report back to the public.

The genetic revolution promises to be every bit as turbulent as the digital revolution, perhaps more so. We still have time to brace ourselves.

vii.

technorealism

*Seeking a Less Divisive Approach to
Understanding and Discussing Technology*

A Philosophy for the Rest of Us

I finally realized for sure that something was wrong with our national conversation about technology late last spring when I slipped on some headphones in a radio studio at KPFA in Berkeley, California, and listened to the host introduce me in this way:

"David Shenk is here with us this morning. He's written a book called *Data Smog* which basically says that the Internet is a giant hoax."

After I had picked my jaw up off the floor and reassembled it, I did my best to politely correct the host. In fact, I am very enthusiastic about the Internet, and about the information revolution. But there are important drawbacks to the proliferation in the speed and volume of information. And it's going to be terribly important for everyone to come to grips with these unintended consequences of hypercommunication if we're going to fully enjoy its benefits.

Unfortunately, my KPFA experience has been all-too-representative of the way people in the media tend to react to a nuanced analysis of how technology affects culture. The latest example is the promotional campaign for the new "Circuits" section of the New York Times: *Are you a technophile or a technophobe?* It makes for a snappy line, but somehow misses the 99 percent of us who would be more accurately described as neither. Most of us approach technology with a mixture of appreciation and skepticism.

Part of the problem, perhaps, is that there's no shorthand phrase for this more nuanced position. Millions of us have been living according to its tenets, but no one has bothered to formalize it.

This is what my friend Andrew Shapiro and I were talking about over lunch last fall. Shapiro, a contributing editor to *The Nation* and a fellow at Harvard's Berkman Center for Internet and Society, is writing an important book about how to protect the public interest in this age of hyperautonomy. The wonderful thing about information technology is that it transfers control from large organizations to individuals. But that's also the problem with technology. Not everything is best left up to market incentives and local or individual control. Important aspects of our health, safety, justice, and economic and political stability must be entrusted to public officials—public servants—who work to maintain larger social interests on our behalf.

After a series of lunches and email exchanges, Andrew and I decided that we should try to articulate this more balanced approach and give it a name. So we did: technorealism. With the help of Steven Johnson, the editor of *Feed* magazine, we drafted a set of principles that we hope will move the conversation forward. Nine other writers —David Bennahum, Brooke Shelby Biggs, Marisa Bowe, Paulina Borsook, Simson Garfinkel, Douglas Rushkoff, Mark Stahlman, Steve Silberman, and Stefanie Syman—have helped us polish up this document and have agreed to lend their names to it so that we could help launch it into the world with some vigor.

A few days ago, we posted "Technorealism: An Overview" on the web. It can be found at www.technorealism.org. Technorealism is by no means an exclusive club. We have invited who anyone feels comfortable with its principles to add their name to our list. Join us.

[Posted to the Technorealism web page, www.technorealism.org,
March 12, 1998]

Technorealism: An Overview

In this heady age of rapid technological change, we all struggle to maintain our bearings. The developments that unfold each day in communications and computing can be thrilling and disorienting. One understandable reaction is to wonder: Are these changes good or bad? Should we welcome or fear them?

The answer is both. Technology is making life more convenient and enjoyable, and many of us healthier, wealthier, and wiser. But it is also affecting work, family, and the economy in unpredictable ways, introducing new forms of tension and distraction, and posing new threats to the cohesion of our physical communities.

Despite the complicated and often contradictory implications of technology, the conventional wisdom is woefully simplistic. Pundits, politicians, and self-appointed visionaries do us a disservice when they try to reduce these complexities to breathless tales of either high-tech doom or cyber-elation. Such polarized thinking leads to dashed hopes and unnecessary anxiety, and prevents us from understanding our own culture.

Over the past few years, even as the debate over technology has been dominated by the louder voices at the extremes, a new, more balanced consensus has quietly taken shape. This document seeks to articulate some of the shared beliefs behind that consensus, which we have come to call technorealism.

Technorealism demands that we think critically about the role that tools and interfaces play in human evolution and everyday life. Integral to this perspective is our understanding that the current tide of technological transformation, while important and powerful, is actually a continuation of waves of change that have taken place throughout history. Looking, for example, at the history of the automobile, television, or the telephone—not just the devices but the institutions they became—we see profound benefits as well as substantial costs. Similarly, we anticipate mixed blessings from today's emerging technologies, and expect to forever be on guard for unexpected consequences—which must be addressed by thoughtful design and appropriate use.

As technorealists, we seek to expand the fertile middle ground between techno-utopianism and neo-Luddism. We are technology "critics" in the same way, and for the same reasons, that others are food critics, art critics, or literary critics. We can be passionately optimistic about some technologies, skeptical and disdainful of others. Still, our goal is neither to champion nor to dismiss technology, but rather to understand it and apply it in a manner more consistent with basic human values.

Below are some evolving basic principles that help explain technorealism.

PRINCIPLES OF TECHNOREALISM

1. Technologies are not neutral.

A great misconception of our time is the idea that technologies are completely free of bias—that because they are inanimate artifacts, they don't promote certain kinds of behaviors over others. In truth, technologies come loaded with both intended and unintended social, political, and economic leanings. Every tool provides its users with a particular manner of seeing the world and specific ways of interacting with others. It is important for each of us to consider the biases of various technologies and to seek out those that reflect our values and aspirations.

2. The Internet is revolutionary, but not utopian.

The Net is an extraordinary communications tool that provides a range of new opportunities for people, communities, businesses, and government. Yet as cyberspace becomes more populated, it increasingly resembles society at large, in all its complexity. For every empowering or enlightening aspect of the wired life, there will also be dimensions that are malicious, perverse, or rather ordinary.

3. Government has an important role
to play on the electronic frontier.

Contrary to some claims, cyberspace is not formally a place or jurisdiction separate from Earth. While governments should respect the rules and customs that have arisen in cyberspace, and should not stifle this new world with inefficient regulation or censorship, it is foolish to say that the public has no sovereignty over what an errant citizen or fraudulent corporation does online. As the representative of the people and the guardian of democratic values, the state has the right and responsibility to help integrate cyberspace and conventional society.

Technology standards and privacy issues, for example, are too important to be entrusted to the marketplace alone. Competing software firms have little interest in preserving the open standards that are essential to a fully functioning interactive network. Markets encourage innovation, but they do not necessarily ensure the public interest.

4. Information is not knowledge.

All around us, information is moving faster and becoming cheaper to acquire, and the benefits are manifest. That said, the proliferation of data is also a serious challenge, requiring new measures of human discipline and skepticism. We must not confuse the thrill of acquiring or distributing information quickly with the more daunting task of converting it into knowledge and wisdom. Regardless of how advanced our computers become, we should never use them as a substitute for our own basic cognitive skills of awareness, perception, reasoning, and judgment.

5. Wiring the schools will not save them.

The problems with America's public schools—uneven funding, social promotion, bloated class size, crumbling infrastructure, lack of standards—have almost nothing to do with technology. Consequently, no amount of technology will lead to the educational revolution prophesied by President Clinton and others. The art of teaching cannot be replicated by computers, the Net, or "distance learning." These tools can, of course, augment an already high-quality educational experience. But to rely on them as any sort of panacea would be a costly mistake.

6. Information wants to be protected.

It's true that cyberspace and other recent developments are challenging our copyright laws and frameworks for protecting intellectual property. The answer, though, is not to scrap existing statutes and principles. Instead, we must update old laws and interpretations so that information receives roughly the same protection it did in the context of old media. The goal is the same: to give authors sufficient control over their work so that they have an incentive to create, while maintaining the right of the public to make fair use of that information. In neither context does information want "to be free." Rather, it needs to be protected.

7. The public owns the airwaves; the public should benefit from their use.

The recent digital spectrum giveaway to broadcasters underscores the corrupt and inefficient misuse of public resources in the arena of technology. The citizenry should benefit and profit from the use of public frequencies, and should retain a portion of the spectrum for educational, cultural, and public access uses. We should demand more for private use of public property.

8. Understanding technology should be an essential component of global citizenship.

In a world driven by the flow of information, the interfaces—and the underlying code—that make information visible are becoming enormously powerful social forces. Understanding their strengths and limitations, and even participating in the creation of better tools, should be an important part of being an involved citizen. These tools affect our lives as much as laws do, and we should subject them to a similar democratic scrutiny.

A Few Moments with Esther Dyson

Dyson is host of the industry conference PC Forum, chairwoman of the Electronic Frontier Foundation, editor of the influential newsletter Release 1.0, *and author of* Release 2.0: A Design for Living in the Digital Age. *When technorealism was first introduced, we carelessly and inadvertently lumped her in with the "cyber-utopians," for which I later apologized. I now understand that Esther is keenly aware of the unintended social consequences of technology, and is always careful to qualify her inherent optimism with some intelligent words of caution.*

DAVID SHENK: The way I've come to think about my role as a technology critic—it's not really about listing the advantages and disadvantages of each machine, but more a matter of articulating the trade-offs that people make in choosing one technology over another.

ESTHER DYSON: Yes, exactly. The biggest challenge is educating people to understand those trade-offs so that they can make the right decisions. There's a downside to anything taken to excess. We've had until now a culture of scarcity. Most of our social problems in the U.S. are now problems of abundance. The problem is now limiting yourself.

DS: There's also an addictive quality to the new speed of information that subverts people's ability to exert discipline.

ED: That's very true. It's like sugar. It is more addictive because it's immediate. But it's less valuable. It is easier to watch eye candy than to watch something with real information in it. What really disturbs me is how everything is becoming entertainment. People are spending the time with mindless information tidbits rather than real information content.

DS: And at the same time, there is the danger of splintering into such specialized communities that we lose touch with people who aren't exactly like us.

ED: The Net is a very good way of creating communities with their own norms. The corresponding danger is fragmentation—people who are totally divorced from reality, forming communities and reinforcing the group's delusions. "Heaven's Gate" is the worst and most visible example of this.

DS: So it's important to resist the temptation to spend all your time in narrow spheres?

ED: Very important. Read stuff you disagree with. Watch a TV show that annoys you. This is why I live in New York—so that I can get on the subway and run into people who are speaking Spanish or who have a different skin color. This is why I'm not driving around in a car in Silicon Valley.

DS: The media is gearing everything to the marketplace. How can we combat this trend?

ED: Write a good book [laughs]. The answer is to complain, to say, "This can't happen. This is wrong." To educate people not just in school. And be annoying. Don't be afraid to say things that are going to make people feel slightly uncomfortable.

[*Feed*, December 3, 1998]

Know Thy Motherboard

Hooray for David Macaulay's
The New Way Things Work

There is a marvelously potent moment, early on in the conversation famously documented a decade ago between Bill Moyers and Joseph Campbell, where the journalist-theologian charmingly parries a question from the professor-mythologist.

> *Campbell:* It's a miracle, what happens on that [computer] screen. Have you ever looked inside one of those things?
>
> *Moyers:* No. And I don't intend to.

The tone is playful, but the remark is a lot more revealing than Moyers probably intended. Is there anyone as well known for open-ended curiosity as he? It's not overreaching, I think, to call Bill Moyers a symbol of the eternally curious, enlightened Western individual. It is his—and our culture's—conceit that such a restless inquisitiveness fuels social enlightenment, and that willful ignorance, its antithesis, is the very root of bigotry.

And yet here is Moyers baring his cerebral Achilles'. *I don't want to know about that.* Here is the one subject to which he would apparently like to shut his eyes: the inner workings of technology.

Honestly, who can blame him? I've said as much hundreds of times to myself and others over the years, and have heard it echoed back from virtually everyone I know. In his reluctance to go under the hood of a computer, Moyers speaks for the vast majority of us who are intimidated by the complexity of the tools we eagerly use. And yet, I'm sure that Moyers intuitively understands as well as anyone the importance of not looking away from microchips. As Marshall McLuhan writes, "Any extension, whether of skin, hand, or foot, affects the whole psychic and social complex."

Go back another decade or so to locate the literary figure who best exemplifies our social alienation from the functioning of machines.

"It's just a whole other thing," Sylvia tells the narrator of Robert Pirsig's *Zen and the Art of Motorcycle Maintenance.* She and her husband John have a deep-seated aversion to trying to understand the workings of their BMW R60 motorcycle and other machines in their life. Pirsig's book is, among other things, a meditative critique of this pervasive attitude. He calls John and Sylvia "spectators" of technology, and wonders if examining "that strange separation of what man is from what man does [may hold] some clues as to what the hell has gone wrong in this twentieth century."

The strange separation *I* confront whenever I revisit *Zen* is the disconnect between my heartfelt agreement with Pirsig and my unwitting alignment with John and Sylvia. It's a point of pretty serious personal disappointment that in the fifteen years since I first read Pirsig's book (and discussed it for months on end with my friend John over sloppy pool shots while multiple tape decks exchanged recordings of Dead shows in the background), my interactions with machines have become less, not more, like those of the book's enlightened narrator. I am surrounded by, and have come to reflexively depend on, machines that I don't really understand—and most of the time don't really even *want* to understand.

We've all read breathy tales of atoms and bits in *Wired,* but who can say how a hard drive or CD player actually works? What about a quartz, or digital, watch? How many of the eight million people in New York City could explain the basic dynamics of an AM radio, let alone a cellular phone? What a strange world we have built: a world full of knowledge, yes, but not shared—only applied; mechanical knowledge so specialized that even technicians can no longer fix machines (mostly they throw them away); where the only thing a consumer can reliably be expected to know about a machine is the terms of its warranty. We are so detached from how our tools actually operate that it has become difficult to continue to think of them as *tools;* they are *electronics* now. Even as they sit on our desks and our wrists, they are the Other, treated at first with reverence, then indifference, and finally—when the electric magic suddenly and inexplicably ceases in the middle of an important meeting or download—with repugnance.

We flock to these machines because they are irresistible, allowing us to do things we couldn't do before, giving us previously unimaginable speed and mobility. They make us superhuman, and no matter how inured we eventually become to their dazzling abilities, we still carry around in our subconscious the sense that without them we'd be no different from the schlumps we see in daguerreotype photographs at flea markets. What we gain in convenience and control, though, we lose in cohesion. In a few moments, I'll print out a draft of this essay on my laser printer. If it were fifteen years ago, I would be striking a simple typewriter key, more or less fully aware of, and viscerally connected to, the mechanical process from beginning to end. Today, I couldn't even begin to explain to myself or my child how the characters will get from my fingers to that paper.

One hesitates to declare that a single 400-page book can deliver salvation, but David Macaulay's *The New Way Things Work* is clearly an antidote to our society's growing technological alienation. The first edition, published ten years ago (and entitled, simply, *The Way Things Work*), was a tour de force, and the book is even more vital now. *The New Way* contains eighty pages in updates, almost all of which appear in a new section, "The Digital Domain." The first page of that section brings the book's cartoon mascot Mammoth to imposing entrance gates controlled by a guy named Bill. The gag is obvious, but since the book is as much aimed at ten-year-olds as it is at thirty-year-olds, Macaulay understandably hammers it home. "So it came to pass," he writes after describing their meeting, "that Mammoth, who generally distrusted high walls, warily entered Bill's gates."

Inside this new domain, Mammoth goes on to discover, by way of elementary concepts and cleverly contextualized illustrations, precisely what happens after someone's index finger presses an "N" on a computer keyboard, how information is transmitted, processed, and stored, how it travels from the computer to a laser printer, and how that signal is turned into an N-shaped inkblot on a piece of paper. There are also marvelous explanations of a mouse/trackball, screen icons, scanners, flash memory, modem, global positioning systems, and virtually any other device you might come into contact with in your daily routine.

How should one read *The New Way*? This book is that rare reference volume that is actually designed to be read in linear fashion, with an explanation of how a pen spits out ink built on the knowledge established on the previous page by an explanation of how a carburetor spits out gasoline. But going backward from just about any point—say from Disk Drive on page 283 back to Maglev Train on page 282, back to Electric Motor, back to Magnetic Attraction, and so on—can work just as well. Personally, I haven't decided if I want to keep it on my desk to satisfy my most impulsive brand of curiosity, beside my bed for nightly digests on how my world functions, or on my living room bookshelf next to secular bibles like the *Oxford English Dictionary*. I've also considered putting it next to my tool bucket, since that's where I often go when I really need to understand why something isn't working.

I do know that when my daughter is old enough to understand what a lever is, I'd like to have a copy in her room so that we can learn about some of this stuff together. And perhaps copies for my parents' homes as well. It's important that Macaulay has created a book that speaks to such a wide variety of ages—and not just because it's nice to have a family media product that doesn't have the Disney stamp on it. This is a book that can catalyze so many meaningful conversations; a six-year-old wanders downstairs and tiptoes into her grandfather's basement workshop. "Granddaddy, how does that old clock always know the right time?" Granddaddy reaches up to the shelf, unfolds his reading glasses. "Well, let's take a look here. . . ."

If that six-year-old never asks such questions, or asks but doesn't get any decent answers, there is much to lose. Our extraordinary ability to communicate nuances of information is one of the very few things that distinguishes humans from other primates. When that thread begins to fray, the consequences can be catastrophic. History shows conclusively that the less people understand about their surroundings, the more vulnerable they are to political subjugation, psychic alienation, and mass hysteria. It's difficult to believe that a society as intensely rational as that of the United States is today could unravel because its technology is *too* sophisticated, but then again, who would have believed fifty-three-and-a-half years ago that any reasonable nation would build a bomb that could destroy the planet?

In fact, evidence mounts that our contemporary rationality is perhaps just a veneer. Remarking on the current surge in beliefs in telekinesis, alien landings, bogus historical revisions, conspiracy theories, and other sundry pseudoscience, religious historian Peter Clark recently declared ours "the most superstitious age ever." Carl Sagan's final book *The Demon-Haunted World* addressed this problem, and the Pope is currently preparing an encyclical on the subject. There are reports that an increasing number of people are forgoing immunization because they believe it is a government plot and doesn't work anyway. Belief in the supernatural and a corresponding repudiation of science both coincide with an understandable awe of the (technological) Other.

Can any one book keep up with the acceleration of change? Thankfully, there are a few others taking on the challenge to explain our most current machines to us. Danny Hillis's *The Pattern on the Stone*, an elegant overview of how software and microchips work, is an important new contribution to this tiny but critical field. But in composing a book that starts with the inclined plane and builds up, Macaulay has created something which is timeless. Sure, by the time my daughter and I can read *A New Way* together, maybe we'll skip over the record player and a few other relics (if Macaulay hasn't edited them out by then). But even as a tool or two drops out of relevance, the work itself won't be in much of danger of obsolescence. As the world becomes based on even more sophisticated machinery, Macaulay's fundamentals are just going to become more and more important to understand. Society will be more advanced, and yet citizens will have even less of an understanding of—and emotional connection to—the real sources of food, electricity, images, sounds, and materials that sustain us. Virtual reality may or may not become a way of life in the future, but either way, we know that there will be more and more of a virtual quality to our physical reality—real buttons and switches replaced by iconic representations of buttons and switches. McLuhan said that all technologies are extensions of our own selves; but what happens when the extensions are so foreign to us that we no longer recognize ourselves? I hope we never find out.

Epilogue

Here Is Tokyo (Irrashaimase!)

Here is Tokyo, the capital of Japan. Twenty-seven million people, give or take. Are you passing through Shinjuku station near 8 A.M.? Good luck to you.

Breakfast—no time. We are sleeping off our sake-then-beer-then-whisky from last night's yakitori-then-ramen-then-karaoke. We are rushing off to work from our two-hour commute train. Grab a cold can of Boss coffee, a bun with sweet bean paste, a cigarette. You don't smoke? Don't be ridiculous—it's 1999, everyone in Tokyo smokes.

Lunch is *kaitenzushi.* Colorful plates of shiny clams, toro rolls, and sliced yellowtail float around the room on a silent conveyor belt. The fish is fresh and the prices are working-class. Eat as much as you please, at your own pace, accompanied by cups of hot green tea and mounds of sweet pickled ginger. Lose yourself in the solitary eating experience.

Now a phone rings, but whose? Yours? Hands flutter for suit pockets and briefcases, and then, before you've found your own phone, the fellow right next to you leans forward into his miso soup and mutters, "Moshi moshi." It's 1999, everyone in Tokyo is wireless.

In fact, cell phones are so popular here, it presents an acute problem for the industry: there's no more room for growth. Nearly everyone in Tokyo who can use a phone—teenagers, salarymen, housewives—already owns one. Industry's instinctive response to cell phone glut: planned obsolescence, a "third generation" of wireless phones, with integrated audio, video, and text, coming soon to an electronics shop near you.

Dinner—well, that depends on how much money, how much time you have. Cold buckwheat soba noodles, a small plate of tempura, and a cold glass of Sapporo will more than satisfy. Maybe, though, you'll be lucky enough to meet up with M—, an old friend of Bill Gates who hasn't done so bad for himself either. It's hard to say where M—will take you. He takes me to Kitcho. In a private room, we drink green tea, a velvety cold sake, and a rich Bordeaux; we eat steamed ginkgo nut, roasted chestnut, crab and caviar, smoked mackerel, grilled matsutake mushroom, toro, sea bream, tender matsutake beef, steamed taro, quail soup, fish tempura, yuba, persimmon, and melon.

In Tokyo, old women sweep the sidewalks every day, cars are cleaned and polished every week, and taxi and bus drivers wear white gloves. Subways are clean, quiet, quick, on time. Things work here.

And yet, strangely, the city has very few street names, and no navigable addresses. Introductory meetings rely on personalized maps, with routes based on visual landmarks. What's your fax number?

Don't be late for a Tokyo appointment. If you are late—well, just don't be. If you are early, apologize. *Osokunatte sumimasen.*

Do you like television? You've come to the right town. Tokyo has tiny TVs in taxis and trains, giant TVs looming over street corners, even "eye-trek" television goggles. Bars, lounges, reception rooms are all drenched in rapid-fire video images. It's as if the entire culture is terrified of going stale.

You are here to observe technology, so you must go to Akihabara, the electric city. Akihabara began as an informal trading post for engineers from a nearby university to scrounge for radio and other basic electronics parts after the war. Now it is perhaps the most intense retail technology market in the world. Under a JR train station in the

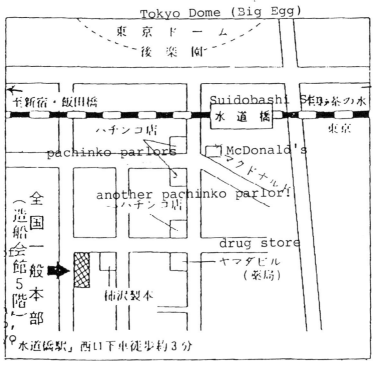

northeast part of town, the first generation of Akihabara still thrives: a lively bazaar of endless cramped stalls, each specializing in variations of one specialty item: diodes, transistors, tubes, switches, adapters, jacks. Here are old radios, computers, phones, screens, lenses, casings, latches, locks, processors, disk drives, hard drives, keyboards, and on, so neatly stacked and ordered that the color patterns and contrasts are soothing in an almost spiritual way. In a city where things work, here is why they work.

Outside the narrow, low-slung hallways, a more contemporary Akihabara of discount electronics and appliance stores sprawls for blocks in every direction. It's a mecca of instant data gratification, the thrill of contact and personalized electrical impulses delivered by the newest of the new watches, cameras, palmtops, handy phones, digicams, global positioning systems, and so on, all priced to move before the new models arrive the week after next. A shopper gazes on an iMac the way Homer Simpson drools over a meatball hoagie. The next great thing is here, and over there, and over there. *You won't believe what this little device can do.* In Akihabara, you'll see not just the smallest television, but also the thinnest. Sony is proud to introduce the "Plasmatron," a giant wide-screen TV you can hang on your wall like a painting (echoes of Ray Bradbury's *Fahrenheit 451*).

Tokyo is current, has no choice but to be current. Obliterated two times in this century alone (earthquake/fire, war), this city does not look over its shoulder. A major fault line runs right along the coastline; massive quakes hit every seventy years like clockwork. The last one was in 1923. Do the math, but keep quiet about it. Look around—it's hard to find anything that predates the last quake. Will the elevated highways survive? The glass towers and electric glass doors? Subways and gas lines? Not surprisingly, the only people willing to discuss any of this are Americans stationed here temporarily. For them, at least it's an "if."

No surprise, then, that Tokyo is constructed like a Lego set; whatever seems to make sense at the moment is built quickly, efficiently. Architecture is either unapologetically raw—luxurious homes with concrete exteriors—or self-consciously eccentric: jigsaw office buildings that slant, or have giant holes in them, or are horseshoe shaped; a convention center is constructed as an upside-down pyramid on fifty-foot stilts, surrounded by a concourse of steel and glass mesh.

In a city this charged, though, it may be that conventional architecture no longer really matters. Static architecture is fast being covered by a Plasmatron and neon veneer, a fluid electric architecture not unlike what Ridley Scott imagined in the futuristic film *Blade Runner*. Outdoor television intrudes on public space, wipes out any potential for deep feeling or connection to the past, replaces it with a forty-foot image of snowboarders in Oregon. Boredom hasn't got a chance here. At Shibuya, Roppongi, Shinjuku, and Ginza, the giant screens constantly interrupt conversation between friends, poke solitary individuals out of their introspection, draw all attention away from the rest of the environment. Never, of course, do the screens contain anything of actual significance, and rarely do people stay long enough to see an entire narrative sequence. It is interruption for interruption's sake.

On smaller sets inside homes, kids watch *Pokemon*, the TV show whose rapid burst of images induced convulsions in more than twelve thousand people one December day in 1997. A few months later, the show was back on the air with a slightly slower flicker rate.

Tokyo, a city with little observable past and no assured future: the perfect staging ground for the final victory of consumerism over other more dated religions. Zen Buddhism, with its ideology of introspection and simplicity, is no match. Consumerism promotes buying as a catharsis, where the most important object or electronic impulse is always the *next* one, the one being yearned for. In the consumerist world, purchasing is advertised as an act which leads to emotional fulfillment. Speed is the ultimate virtue in the consumer realm. TV and all venues of consumerism aim to convince people to make snap decisions. Any sort of introspection or meditation is strongly discouraged in this electric atmosphere, because such an approach would deconstruct and usually destroy the buying impulse.

So there is Tokyo. Kyoto, three hours away by train, stands in contrast, gives new meaning to the word *contrast*. This former capital was spared Allied bombing in World War II (including a last-moment reprieve from Secretary of War Henry Stimson that made Hiroshima and not Kyoto the target of the first atom bomb). In Kyoto, you may stroll through mossy gardens and even stay in wooden inns (*ryokan*) that are centuries old. The slower pace and connection to the past is no tourist gimmick; you can feel the stillness of the air here. There is time and space to think. Plunge into a cedar tub full of hot water. Sit on the steps of an old temple and contemplate the rock garden in front of you. Step over a narrow stone bridge and marvel at the giant golden and yellow *koi* eyeing you from the water. Kyoto is not without its rampant consumerism (just as Tokyo has contemplative spaces). But here in Kyoto, at least, one can see the battle lines drawn between the old world and the new. A man is race-walking through the green stillness of Honen-in temple chattering on a cell phone. What more perfect image of the clear and present danger: that people will become so addicted to the pulse of electronic communication, trafficking in the latest data updates, that they will become oblivious to serenity—oblivious, even, to history.

Name Index

about the author

David Shenk is author of *Data Smog* and co-author (with Steve Silberman) of *Skeleton Key*. He has written for *Harper's*, *Wired*, the *New York Times*, and the *New Yorker*, and is an occasional commentator for NPR's "All Things Considered." Shenk was a 1995–1996 Freedom Forum Media Studies Fellow and a 1998 U.S.–Japan Fellow. He lives in Brooklyn with his wife and daughter, and is currently at work on a book about Alzheimer's disease.